SMILE OF THE UNIVERSE

MIRACLES IN AN AGE OF DISBELIEF

MICHAEL GROSSO, PhD

ANOMALIST BOOKS
*San Antonio * Charlottesville*

An Original Publication of ANOMALIST BOOKS
Smile of the Universe: Miracles in an Age of Disbelief

ISBN: 978-1-949501-13-1

Cover: “Flash” by Filograph/iStock and “milkyway” by Aperture Vintage/Unsplash

Book Design: Seale Studios

For information about the publisher, go to AnomalistBooks.com, or write to: Anomalist Books, 5150 Broadway #108, San Antonio, TX 78209

Contents

They say miracles are past; and we have our philosophical persons to make modern and familiar things supernatural and causeless. Hence it is we make trifles of terrors, ensconcing ourselves into seeming knowledge, when we should submit ourselves to an unknown fear.

William Shakespeare
All's Well That Ends Well

There was a widespread feeling that the time had come for man to gather all his strength for a flight into some new sphere of mentality. The present type of human being, it was recognized, was but a rough and incoherent natural product. It was time for man to take control of himself and remake himself upon a nobler pattern.

Olaf Stapledon
Last and First Men

Preface

On October 27, 1994, I drove to St. Irene Chrysovalantou Cathedral in Astoria, New York City; I had come to witness a miracle with my own eyes. A small crowd was gathering on the white steps of the Greek Orthodox Church. By the time I turned the corner, parked, and walked back, a line five-abreast and a block long had formed leading up to the steps. The previous evening, thousands had assembled to solemnly walk through the portals of the cathedral.

At the altar was an icon of Saint Irene who lived in the age of Constantinople. About a foot square, it was mounted under glass with an outside kneeler for a person to pray and express devotion. It was reported on NBC's "A Current Affair" the night before that *the icon was shedding tears*. Familiar with the curious history of eyewitness reports of statues, icons, and paintings that weep and bleed, here was my chance to observe the strange phenomenon with my own eyes.

I had to wait about 45 minutes before climbing the cathedral steps. The crowd was orderly and pensive, mostly Greeks from the neighborhood. It is called a cathedral, but once inside I realized how small and intimate it was compared to most Western churches, the walls crowded with paintings and icons and the atmosphere suffused with a warm mystic glow. Celebrants bought candles, thick white ones about three feet long, lighting them for votive purposes.

At first, I doubted I would see anything, the church being poorly lit and the icon set in a darkish enclosure. When my turn came, a woman handed me a candle and I stepped very close. At once I was able to see—without the candle—that several large drops of transparent liquid had formed around the eyes and were trickling down the surface of the icon. There was no question in my mind about the fact that I saw this. I stepped back and walked around the icon, noting its wooden enclosure; no pipes or appurtenances were visible that could account for any accidental leakage.

However, somebody could conceivably have rigged up a device inside the enclosure, causing drops to seep through the icon's surface.

A tall, ruddy-faced, bearded young man in monkish garb was standing beside the icon.

"It's a bad omen," he said, shaking his downcast head.

The image had begun to shed tears 10 days previously on Wednesday, October 17. The icon, which belonged to Saint Irene's for 20 years, was at that time lodged in a sister cathedral in Chicago for the purpose of being blessed. It was during vespers when the congregation was praying for peace in the Middle East that the phenomenon began. It was immediately taken by those present to signify impending catastrophe. Needless to say, the Middle East has been roiling in wars and chaos ever since the American invasion of Iraq.

I asked the priest if anyone had taken a sample of the tears and submitted them to chemical analysis. He looked at me as if I had stabbed him in the back:

"You really want to do that?" he said.

"It would help," I said.

To the pious young priest, the idea of a scientific test was quite beside the point. He said the icon had been the subject of reports of miracles for 14 years, including healings of serious diseases like cancer. He spoke with enthusiasm of the heroic life of the saintly Irene, stressing the torments of her daily struggles with diabolic agents, adding that she had lived to be over a hundred.

A slightly older, plumper man with a stately black beard stepped up. Bishop Vincent was his name. He was the man I had seen on television. I asked him about doing a chemical analysis of the liquids; he agreed it would be a good idea. He said it would be arranged once the proper authorities were called in. He seemed more than willing to comply; for once the enclosure was opened, he was confident further talk of hoaxing would end.

Bishop Vincent explained how the weeping began in Chicago during a prayer for peace in the Middle East. "Did the icon ever shed tears before?" I asked. Once, he said, on the feast day of Saint Irene, August 2, a year ago; it had briefly produced some teardrops. This time the weeping has been more or less continuous for 10 days. The Bishop pointed out that on Friday evening, October 26, after the great crowds had dispersed, the icon became dry. In the morning, the tears began to flow again. Because of this extraordinary behavior, and because of the escalating crisis in the Middle East, the officials decided to parade the icon through the streets of Astoria on Sunday, October 28th. By the way, in Greek the word *irene* means "peace."

It rained lightly that morning. I returned to Saint Irene's Cathedral. Once again the line leading inside was long and wide. The procession would start at 11:30, and ABC television was there to record events. I spoke with a Greek-American man who smiled gently and expressed his skepticism. Harsh sounding chants and words of peace for the Middle East piped from inside the cathedral. According to the doubting Thomas, in 1980 somebody foretold that one day great crowds of people would come to venerate the Miraculous Icon of the Saint of Peace, and that this marvel would transpire in Astoria, New York. (Coincidentally, I was born and raised in Astoria, New York.)

Children in white costumes, nubile lasses and handsome youths in gay colors, priests and bishops in black robes, all waited till the icon was presented on the steps. It had been taken out of the kneeling booth and was raised aloft by two men. The moment the icon, which had now been weeping for 12 days, was brought into view, a hush came upon the crowd. The procession of worshippers followed through the streets and returned to the cathedral steps where the sick waited in hope of healing.

A woman tapped me on the shoulder. She had just come from Saint Demetrios Cathedral, another Greek church a few blocks away. The ushers at Saint Demetrios had told her not to go to Saint Irene's. The so-called miracle was a fake, they insisted, without offering any evidence; it was a trick to make money. Apparently, the pilgrims were buying thousands of dollars worth of candles. Most people were indeed sporting candles, but nobody was forcing them to buy anything. It seemed petty and vindictive for a rival church to encourage such rumors.

Was the icon really weeping? Or were the people of Saint Demetrios right? Did someone rig it to make the drops appear as if from nowhere? But who? The likely suspects would be the bishops and priests in charge. But why would they attempt such a scam with a skeptical press watching them like hawks? I don't blame the skeptic. That tears might materialize from a piece of wood certainly seems incredible. Do statues weep? Do such thoroughly queer anomalies actually occur in this day or age? What to make of such fantastic claims? What I saw with my own eyes, was it a trick, an illusion, tears from Mind at Large—or what?

Introduction

This book is meant to save miracles from the dogmatic clutches of religion and science. Not to say that science and religion have nothing to contribute--on the contrary. But I want to return to the phenomena themselves and not be hampered by the biases of scientists and religionists. One way to explore miracles is through their multiple meanings and historical contexts. A brilliant example of this approach is Kenneth Woodward's *The Book of Miracles* (2000). "Rather than ask, did it really happen?" writes Woodward, he invited "a different question: what does it mean?"

This book is concerned with the fundamental question that Woodward lays aside: *Did it really happen?* In order to get at the various, full meanings of an event, it must make a difference to know that the event actually occurred. The sheer existence and reality of so-called "miracles" must itself be of momentous meaning, especially in a declining culture whose official worldview tends to dismiss the idea of miracles as a holdover from medieval superstition. The question I want to pose: Supposing in fact there are unrecognized but profound human capacities. Suppose we do possess "miraculous" potentials. It would seem only natural to want to explore the subject more deeply.

One thing can be said for asking about the reality of miracles. For the philosopher, or anybody, interested in the nature of mind, miracles afford a feast of counter-examples to the doctrine of materialism, the monistic fantasy that all things can be explained physically. The phenomena focused on in this book will propel us to expand our appreciation of mental reality. I see this latent potential as pointing to the possible development of something like a higher kind or species of humanity. Many of the phenomena we discuss can be seen as snapshots of future developments. What frame of reference is best for thinking futuristically like this remains for me an open question.

Miracles are stories of seemingly "impossible" events, rare to occur no doubt and unpredictable, and usually told in terms provided by the local religion or folk beliefs. And yet (at least) as far back as Shakespeare's day, the "philosophers" were disputing their reality. Modern scientists are just squeamish about the idea of a miracle. Nonetheless, reports of miracles persist and fascinate because they stretch our imagination of what is possible. Others may be happy to see what seems to them ratification of their belief-system, often religious.

However you frame it, you will need an elastic imagination. It may not be easy to digest accounts of instantaneous healings at Lourdes or the ecstatic levitations of Milarepa or Joseph of Copertino, but we will go where more conventional intellectual explorers refuse to go. We will confront the data, see what they are, and what they might mean for us in the 21st century, especially where they promise to take us. The data suggest the need for a new paradigm that abandons physicalism and makes consciousness the keystone of a radically new metaphysics. It will seem to us like signs and illustrations of a single all-pervasive mind that has been named and renamed time and again, understood and interacted with in endlessly nuanced ways. The Indian Rig Veda says it in a spirit of global democracy: "Truth is one; people call it variously."

A Quixotic Quest

A book about miracles in the twenty-first century? In an age of scientific triumphalism? Outlandish, if not ludicrous, especially to more educated people. Miracles are nothing but a kind of balm or mental baby food, some will say. Educated religious believers often beg off from having anything to do with miracles. For most mainstream scientists, especially materialists, the idea of "miracle" is a non-starter. But this may just be "ensconcing ourselves into a seeming knowledge," as Lafeu from Shakespeare's *All's Well That Ends Well* says, that is, assuming we know more than we really do.

There are reasonable, scholarly ways to talk about miracles; and many sides to miracle stories and claims—political, economic, artistic, psychological, and metaphysical. There may be something else of importance. We are told by Socrates in Plato's *Theatetus* that wonder is the beginning (*arche*) of philosophy. To wonder is to feel the spur to seek new knowledge and perhaps greater wisdom. Miracles, or even apparent miracles, are apt to excite wonder and stir the intellectual imagination.

As a teenager, I wrote down three questions that puzzled me. The first was about the sheer fact of anything at all existing. I knew nothing of Leibniz who famously asked: "Why is there something rather than nothing?" The second puzzler was that I was alive—as a teenager I couldn't help noticing that I was. I wondered—how did living beings manage to emerge from dead things? And the third item that zapped my budding intellect: I wanted to know how the piece of star dust I was became *conscious*. I still wonder at this trio of questions about being, life, and consciousness. With a little luck, the phenomena covered in the present book will ease some of my cognitive aches and pains—and perhaps yours. On the other hand, they might increase them.

Religious traditions, world literature, mythology, folktales, and the like, all are rich in miracle lore. Belief in miracles seems an ingrained need of imagination; to banish them all with a wave of the hand would be a crime against the spirit. For one thing, apparent miracles have played a major role in the birth of most religions. But before we go on with examples, let's get clear on our use of the term.

An Attempt at Definition

According to Skeat's *Etymological Dictionary*, the word *miracle* is rooted in a Sanskrit syllable *smi*, from which we get the English word *smile*. *Miracle* refers to a smile of a type induced by certain sensations of awe, beauty, and wonder. Etymology brings us back to the concrete origins of words that have otherwise in time become vague and abstract.

Extraordinary experiences do indeed make us smile with wonder; but they also make us ask questions, think new thoughts, and explore novel possibilities. As evident from history, different traditions have different ways of naming, describing, and enshrining their importance. In this book, the focus is mainly on what the miracle is said to do, less on how it is interpreted, mythically or theologically.

A miracle, as I use the term, is an event that parapsychologists call *paranormal*, but of a particular type: *miracles are paranormal events that occur in the context of religious belief, symbols, and experience*. In a broader, looser sense, I will use the term to refer to any event that *prima facie* is physically unexplained, as with non-religious paranormal phenomena, a category much wider than the mainly religious. The "religious" category of miracles includes many of the most provocative and mysterious phenomena. By the term *paranormal* one refers to events that are "para" or *beyond* any type of known physical causation. Religious miracles are associated with ascetic practices, sanctity, prayer, fasting, grace, or possibly sheer luck. In the language of myth and archetype, miracles are charged with *numinous* power; fascinating and awe-inspiring, they may transform people, indeed whole movements and cultures.

Our definition makes no assumptions about the cause of miracles; it is openly provisional in that regard. It saves the idea that miracles signify a break from ordinary reality and possibly point to a transcendent mode of existence. Like the term *paranormal*, miracle denotes a fracture in the causal chain of our familiar world; a region of uncertainty, of mystery, perhaps of transcendence. The definition preserves the extraordinary and numinous associations of the word without committing itself to dubious theological or scientific assumptions—the existence of a particular God, for example, or the belief that a natural law has been *violated*. As far as I can see, the phenomena of miracles violate nothing but intellectual provincialism.

We meet all manner of reported events on their face unexplained, often shocking and sometimes heartfelt and moving. Their exact ontological status may remain obscure but the impact of their being or even seeming miraculous will remain. One curious example is having a close call with death, just missing some disaster; it will typically feel like divine intervention.

There are loose but also precise theological senses of the word. It is normal usage to speak of the miracles of science, of natural beauty, of the human heart. Miracles, as suggested by the title of this book, are the "smiles" of the universe – events that stop, perplex, amaze, fascinate, terrify, and also amuse us. Some miracles are truly bizarre. Take, for example, the Convulsionaries of St. Medard whose grotesque jaw-dropping behaviors were repeatedly observed.[1] Another example is the image of Joseph of Copertino literally flying over the heads of the Spanish Viceroy and his "vehement" wife as a ploy to avoid having to talk with them! That's as funny as anything the Marx Brothers ever did.

Miracles are supposed to knock us out of complacency. St. Augustine thought the existence of the universe was a miracle. There might just as well have been nothing; that there is *anything at all* is cause for wonder. "And a mouse," said Walt Whitman, "is miracle enough to stagger sextillions of infidels." Still others might say with reason that every true act of love, forgiveness, or courage is a miracle. To father and mother, the sight of their newborn infant's face is apt to fill them with a sense of grateful awe and wonder. And so on. We should honor the subjective sense of the word, but there are more precise senses I want to tease out and specify for use in our story.

St. Augustine wrote: "Miracles happen, not in opposition to nature, but in opposition to what we know of nature." What we call a miracle today may be brought into the fold of familiar lawlike nature tomorrow. As we proceed, example by example, the invitation is to imagine how we may or could be unfolding the extraordinary potential implied by these powers. Some thinkers have viewed miracles as extensions of nature. John Scotus Erigena (a philosopher born in Ireland around 810) expanded the idea of nature to include everything under the concept of the spiritual and the miraculous: "For nothing that can be thought of as obtaining in the universe would remain outside this designation."[2]

Like Augustine, John Scotus sensed that nature itself is rich in miraculous potential; but the Synod of Valence found the latter's ideas too dangerous for orthodoxy and condemned many of his theses. He believed, for example, that even the most evil people were eventually absorbed back into the divine bosom; like the ancient Zoroastrians, he was a cosmic optimist. This generous eschatology was not received with joy; the chroniclers report that he was stabbed to death by an irate mob of students.

Obvious Miracles

Before heading out into the exotic zones, let me say a few words about what I call *obvious* miracles. There are certain things we're all acquainted with and take for granted that established science cannot yet explain. Despite the great advances of neuroscience, chemistry, and physics, on many scientific fronts we remain flanked by mysteries. We don't have to travel far to find them. All we need do is turn our attention inward, and we find ourselves immersed in a reality whose nature is quite different from that of the physical world: our thoughts, feelings, moods, willings, memories, dreams, images, and visions are invisible, intangible, subjective, and utterly unlike the public, physically measurable things in the external world of space and time.

The American philosopher and psychologist William James thought the emergence of consciousness from brain matter would be nothing short of "miraculous."[3] Contemporary philosophers speak of consciousness as "the hard problem" while the British philosopher Colin McGinn argues that consciousness is irreducibly mysterious.[4] Our brains are not equipped to fathom the miracle of conscious existence; so there is a *mysterian* aspect of reality itself, an irreducible datum.[5] Consciousness, of course, is an especially hard problem if you try to explain it physically. Failing that, we are bound to acknowledge consciousness as a fundamental feature of reality, a mode of being unto itself.

Consciousness has many aspects, many dimensions. Take something we all know and use, and upon which our knowledge and self-identity depend—memory.[6] Despite the efforts of neuroscientists and the analytic jugglings of philosophers, memory remains a riddle if not a mystery. Memories don't seem localized very specifically in the brain but rather seem to deploy the whole brain in a way that suggests the mind uses the brain and can in fact mold and rewire its structure.[7] Matter and memory are related but not identical. Our capacity to be aware, to doubt, to choose, to morally act cannot be explained in terms of physical mechanisms because their operations are not in three-dimensional space. The freedom of the creative imagination is another headache for anyone who would reduce the subtleties of mind to physical processes.

The list of insurgents grows. We have said nothing of the commonplace mysteries of dreams, clearly "miraculous" in their phenomenal epiphanies and archetypal power. In some ways, dreams are the greatest among commonplace mysteries; they create transient worlds of experience, fashion from an invisible storehouse all manner of convincingly real experiences of psychic reality. Nothing could be more commonplace and nothing could be more astonishing. Also perfectly ordinary are deep puzzles about pain, about the well-studied placebo effect, and about the odd fact of our persistent self-identity in the midst of constant bodily change and sensory flux. Nor should we omit the origin of life in our list of the radically unexplained. A great deal that is obvious and nearby is cloaked in mystery.

On the other hand, when we turn to the microphysical, the quantum world, it appears that matter becomes more mindlike, more dematerialized, more akin to the Void of mystic and Zen master.[8] So, for wonder-lovers, the quantum realm is what the Danish physicist Niels Bohr called "shocking" once we try to understand it. As for the far side of the cosmos, again we run into cognitively shocking scenarios. We are told we know a small percentage of the physical universe. Twenty-five percent is "dark" or invisible matter and 70 percent is dark energy, which is causing the expansion of the universe to accelerate. All this is, in Shakespeare's word, *causeless*—unexplained and leaving us ensconced in certain ignorance. Thus, looking within or looking without, we meet the same smiling face of a universe that is strange and wondrous.

The foregoing lists a few mysteries of things otherwise obvious. But there are also unobvious mysteries. Rummaging through the records of history, folklore, comparative religion, medicine, anthropology, the annals of mesmerism and hypnotism, spiritualism, psychical research, modern parapsychology, ufology, and more, we encounter incidents that qualify, by our extraphysical criteria, as *miraculous*. The word is meant as a reminder of all we don't know.

Our aim here is to dwell on the phenomenology of miracles--disengage the phenomena from their encrusted interpretations and look at them as items of original human experience. Christians say *charisms* or "gifts," implying a God who gives the gifts; yogis of India say *siddhis* or "attainments," understood as byproducts of voluntary effort. (Both metaphors serve a valid purpose.) There is also a contrast between religious and secular characterizations; thus, one might speak of "discernment of spirits" or, more neutrally, of "telepathy" or even "anomalous cognition," adopting, in tone, a cooler minimalist stance.

Overview

Let's glance at the coming highlights. After recording my observations of a weeping statue in New York, in the Preface, and stipulating a working definition of miracle in this Introduction, I provide in Chapter One, "Opening Salvos," some other contemporary accounts of materialization miracles around the world, illustrating the different ways that nature baffles our customary epistemic expectations.

The second chapter, "A Concise Anthology of Miracles," covers a variety of reported cases of phenomena that fit our definition of miracle. Many examples are drawn from the lives of Catholic mystics. We have good reports of these thanks to a tradition of deposing eyewitness testimony for miracle claims. The *processi* or "trials" that document miracles are part of the Church's method of saint-making, a process that keeps evolving; nowadays, for example, experts outside the Church are increasingly brought in to assess miracle claims.[9] However, the accounts in this chapter draw on all cultures and religions. Extraordinary phenomena, rising to the miraculous, seem a constant throughout human history, the content and the modus operandi evolving in context but also displaying universal forms and themes.

Chapter Three, "Beyond Physicalism," covers arguments against miracles, for example, those of David Hume, the Scottish Enlightenment philosopher, historian, economist, and essayist. It calls attention to phenomena evaded by Hume, phenomena widely reported about the Medard Convulsionaries.[10] Also available at that time were the well-attested levitations of the mystics Joseph of Copertino and Teresa of Avila. And while the Enlightenment philosophes were heralding the triumph of mechanistic science, Anton Mesmer, a German doctor, had launched a psychological movement that led to the discovery of new forms of unconscious and super-conscious mental life—to Janet and Freud, Jungian psychology, and psychical research.

From there we move on to Marian visions, Hindu mass miracles of the 20th century, Sai Baba's reported materializations, then to a discussion of Padre Pio as possible model for "future man," Chinese studies of kid's psychokinesis, the disturbing world of angry ghosts, and so on. The chapter points to the range and diversity of miracles, raising questions about fundamental conceptions of reality.

"Things to Do with Miracles," Chapter Four, asks: What are we to do with these metaphysical outliers? To begin with, they are a boon for the faithful, a prophylactic against what the Italian political philosopher and rhetorician Giambattista Vico called the "barbarism of reflection." The faithful believe in the impossible; it turns out that the "impossible" is sometimes a fact of nature. They are also a boon for science; miracles provide a cornucopia of anomalies, exceptions to many rules of mainstream science, and therefore means and motive to advance the cause of science by increasing and expanding knowledge. Then we move on to the world of art and look at miracles as motifs of much great art, but of special interest to Surrealism, in which the project becomes how to combine dream and waking reality to create *surreality*. Last but not least, we can use miracles to stand up against barriers arbitrarily imposed on what we are permitted to think of as possible. We may regard them as an especially potent intellectual tonic.

Chapter Five takes its title, "Living by Miracle," from a phrase by the English poet William Blake. Here we ponder some pointers to how one might learn to "live by miracle." What, concretely and realistically, might that mean? Four possibilities are placed on the table: deep faith, deep introversion, goal-oriented thinking, and spontaneity—a psychically potent foursome.

Chapter Six, "The Hypothesis of Mind at Large," argues for one of the recurrent spiritual intuitions of humankind: the belief that there is "something greater than us," a mind, a spirit, decidedly more powerful than our woefully weak and finite selves. This greater reality goes under many names like God, Goddess, Allah, Providence, World-Soul, Tao, Brahman, Atman, Wakan Tanka, Orenda, Cosmic Consciousness, and so on and so forth. Philosophical and empirical arguments converge that allow us to form an idea of a transcendent mind, a mind at large, all-pervasive and nonlocalized. In my opinion, the data forces us to radically revise the understanding of mind. The revision is decidedly in the direction of expansion so that we may now think in terms of habitual small minds and our latent great mind.

Chapter Seven takes the next step. Suppose indeed that reason and matters of fact convince us of the reality of Mind at Large. We might then ask: Can we engage with this greater mind in some meaningful way? Can we talk to Mind at Large? History provides a resounding reply: At all times people have reached out to elicit guidance, insight, consolation, courage, strength, and inspiration from whatever reputed higher spiritual powers were available through traditional belief systems.

One: Opening Salvos

As it turns out, since my observation of the weeping icon of St. Irene in Astoria, New York, in 1994, I have learned quite a bit more about these exceedingly strangely phenomena. Apparently, the number of reports of tears and blood materializing from religious statues, paintings, and crucifixes is by no means insignificant. And, in fact, along with visions of the Virgin Mary, these materialization phenomena have become global. The evidence for their occurrence is actually on the increase, especially in Italy, and strangely for a largely Protestant country, in certain parts of the U.S.A.[11]

Materializations (and its opposite, dematerializations) are as "shocking" and counter-intuitive as quantum physics is said to be. With materialization, we not only have an unexplained physical occurrence, but the physical objects involved seem to emerge from no known or sensible source. Clearly, they appear to emerge from *nothing* or from another dimension of reality. Either way, our everyday assumptions about how the world works must be in grave error. Materialization is a very mysterious kind of creativity. One thinks of the magical creation stories found everywhere in the annals of religious mythology. Is there some real transcendent power behind the great creation narratives out there?

Let me begin with one striking case that takes us back to the late Middle Ages in 1264. It is the story of a pious German priest who was suffering from doubts about the reality of transubstantiation, the doctrine that the consecrated bread and wine during mass become the actual presence, the body and blood of Jesus, the son of the Abrahamic God. The disturbed priest stopped in Bolsena to celebrate mass in the church of Santa Cristina. At the moment he raised and was about to consecrate the Eucharistic wafer, he prayed to have his doubts about the rite he was performing removed. At that moment the wafer began to bleed! The corporal, a linen cloth on which consecrated objects are laid during mass, collected twenty-five drops of blood. Eventually, the blood-stained corporal was moved to the cathedral in Orvieto and installed into a reliquary and became the basis of a series of striking artworks all designed to memorialize what seemed like proof of the reality of transubstantiation—the reality, in short, of "real magic," as understood by the scientist Dean Radin.[12] It was clearly a response to the priest's prayer. The artworks were the medieval equivalent of modern photographic evidence. What we can agree upon is that a deeply conflicted priest was somehow responsible for the materialization of what looked like blood.

It is possible to accept the story exactly as told, a true account of real events, but give it a psychodynamic, not a religious, interpretation. The experience of the priest is analogous to some poltergeist cases where intolerable psychic conflicts exteriorize in bizarrely expressive ways. The priest's story fits, but his psyche was more focused than the usual bedlam of weird effects associated with poltergeists that emanate from the more chaotic psyches of problem kids.

Moving ahead to May of 1914, Everard Feilding, W. B. Yeats, and Maud Gonne went to Mirebeau, France, to meet with Abbé Vachere. In 1906 the latter was given two pictures (oleographs) of the Sacred Heart. On September 8, 1911, one of these images began to bleed from the forehead where a dark red spot had strangely appeared. Feilding, Yeats, and Gonne witnessed the bleeding and returned at a later date as word of the case spread. Eventually it was confirmed by independent scientists that it was real blood. Other phenomena occurred such as flows of tears from the eyes of Christ. Vachere claimed he saw the lips of the image of Christ open and heard lamentations. As it turned out, a hostile Inquisition excommunicated the priest despite numerous witnesses, including scientists, ratifying the reality of the blood effects.[13]

Abbé Vachere, as do many involved in these epiphanies of blood and tears, saw them as symptoms of dying spiritual power. The numinous effects seem to hover around the one remnant of ancient goddess worship still alive in modern times—the figure of Mary, the Blessed Virgin, whom Coptic Christians call *theotokos*—the "godbearer."

The history of Marian visions and related phenomena such as weeping and bleeding statues is surveyed in Albert J. Hebert's *The Tears of Mary and Fatima. Why?* (1983). He notes that although the phenomenon is global, there seems a concentration of Marian phenomena in Italy and the United States. In spite of themselves, these two countries seem to be in the vanguard of challenging the male-driven capitalist-materialist ethos that's wrecking our planet. That seems the gist of Hebert's message; it's far-fetched, but the point is well made about the growing number of reports of visions, and of tears and blood materializing, all revolving around a numinous feminine figure. It may be in compensation for, and revolt against, the varieties of male domination.

The general culture acknowledges the power of the Marian archetype. A recent issue of *Life* magazine shows a white statue of the Madonna with a child kissing her hand. The whole issue is about miracles and is illustrated with some of the world's great art. Two recent issues of *National Geographic* have portraits of Mary on their covers. The caption on one of them reads: "The Most Powerful Woman in the World." The other issue opens to a detailed global "Map of Mary sightings."

In the study of miracles one type is quite shocking, for it involves materialization, which seem as logically perverse as precognition. How can something come out of nothing? It's a nasty question just like: How can the effect come before the cause? As it turns out, there are stories—I began this book with a case I and a colleague witnessed for ourselves—of images or statues that weep and bleed. These, if authentic, by our definition, qualify as miracles. There was a notable outbreak of such in the 1990s—the decade I was lucky enough to observe the phenomenon. I offer a few examples collected from sources around the world.[14] They affirm historian Philip Jenkins' point about the experiential roots of the rise of the new "Christendom." These are the sort of facts—presuming that's what they are—that add to our ignorance of what is possible in human experience.

And so, in *Santiago, Chile, 1992*, "a six-inch-high porcelain statue began weeping tears of blood. The liquid staining the image was blood, and human at that. The Santiago coroner's office pronounced the substance is type O-4 human blood. The statue wept regularly, particularly in the presence of children," according to the British daily *The Guardian*. Doctors attached to the police Criminal Investigation Department stated that the mysterious red liquid, which flowed from the eyes of a statue of the Virgin Mary belonging to a Chilean woman, is indeed human blood. Dr. Inelia Chacon stated that three samples of the liquid examined in a laboratory were blood. The statue belonged to Olga Rodriguez, a housewife from the working class La Cisterna district of Santiago. Since November 14th, when the tears of blood were seen for the first time, Mrs. Rodriguez' home became the main attraction for residents of the district. The Church, predictably, abstained from taking a position on the phenomenon.

Virginia, 1992: A Catholic parish priest attracted national media attention, as well as thousands of visitors, to the local Catholic church because of eyewitness accounts that around him statues of the Virgin Mary weep tears and blood. It was also said that he had stigmata on his wrists and feet, mirroring the wounds of Christ. The Father James Bruse, an unassuming associate pastor at St. Elizabeth Ann Seton Church in Lake Ridge, Virginia, began experiencing these phenomena, and told the superior who heads the parish. Father Daniel Hamilton reportedly saw the wounds on Bruse's wrists and a statue in Bruse's room produce blood. Since then he has seen the crying and bleeding statues, and Bruse's stigmata, numerous times. He says, "Of course I doubted it in the beginning. But then I saw some of this stuff he'd been talking about. It's true. That's all I can tell you. It's true."

According to parish officials and church parishioners, many times during, before, or after a church service, hundreds in attendance have seen the church's statue of the Virgin Mary cry. Other statues on the parish grounds have been seen to weep as well. After Bruse celebrated Mass at a nearby church, water reportedly began dripping from the church's wooden statue of the Virgin Mary. The phenomena occur irregularly; Bruse sometimes has only to be near the statue for the apparent crying to begin. A *Washington Post* reporter who covered the story and personally witnessed a crying statue while interviewing Bruse wrote, "There's gotta be a trick here. It's as if the water is just appearing right out of the plaster and then rolling downward. Proof positive you can be seeing something and still not believe you're seeing it." Tom Saunders, a local church-goer, has photos of a weeping statue, and says one statue "cried in my hand." Saunders claims he has seen at least a dozen statues cry. "When you see it, it's hard to believe at first," he says. "But it's there."[15]

Ohio, 1992: At a tiny church located in the industrial section of town, people watched a painting of the Virgin Mary weep. At St. Jude Orthodox Church in Barberton, Ohio, tears were reported to flow from the Virgin's eyes on the two-by-three-foot painting. St. Jude's pastor, Father Roman, like many of the visitors to the church, believes the event in Barberton was a miracle, "a sign of compassion from God." Of the painting, he said: "If it gives some blessing, we'd like people to come and see it. We want to try to bring people back to church and God." Miracles, in this context, we can think of as highly expressive symptoms of an ailing psychospiritual organism.

New York, 1994: In the Benson Hurst neighborhood of Brooklyn, New York, witnesses claimed to observe a picture of the Virgin Mary weeping oil. The icon resided in the house of a member of the Egyptian Coptic Orthodox sect. Said one visitor: "If you smell it, it doesn't smell at all. You feel it when you go up to it. You feel a chill going through your body." The oil continued to drip for days and stopped when the picture was transferred to an Egyptian church nearby.[16]

Ireland, 1994: Three thousand pilgrims arrived from all over the world in County Wicklow village of Grangecon, Ireland, to witness a statue of the Madonna that wept blood. In early May, Mrs. Murray, a retired postmistress and her daughter noticed that their statue's eyes had filled with tears and drops of blood trickled from the left eye, leaving a brown stain. Many visitors claim to have seen the eyes water. Most said a sense of peace radiated from the statue. People flocked to see it; Mrs. Murray welcomed travelers from 8am to 11pm every day. To manage the crowds, the statue was moved and placed in the village, as reported in the *Daily Mail*.

Australia, 1994: Every day, dozens of people visited a small home to witness tears flow from the eyes of a statue of Our Lady of Fatima. Sixteen-year-old Sam Scevola from Rooty Hill, near Sydney, bought the statue in an antique shop. Shortly after bringing it home, he and his mother discovered drops of liquid rolling down the statue's face. "It took us a while to realize it was the statue that was sobbing," says Sam. "My mother and I both collapsed when the truth sank in."

The statue's crying has since been so constant that it has forced the Scevolas to place cotton balls between the lady's praying hands and her body to collect the moisture. Church officials were aware of the crying statue, but could not comment until they completed their investigation, according to *The U.S. Sun*.

Italy, 1994: Italian Catholics regard it as a '"miracle"—for from a statue of Christ found by a policeman on the refuse belt of Sant'Antonio Abate near Naples, a red fluid was seen to stream forth. It first appeared in the eyes and then head, hands, breast, and feet. After a report by the Italian TV station RAI-2, thousands of people curious to see it went to Sant'Antonio Abate, creating a traffic jam. All for nothing, as the Bishop of Castelimare di Stabia had removed the statue. And so it went.

And now, in the early 21st century, it seems that cases of materialization, though by no means common, are apparently on the increase.

The foregoing represents a fragment of what is available for further investigation. They describe events that may in a true sense of the word be *surreal*. For the French writer and poet Andre Breton surreal described a situation in which events fuse in a space that mingles dream and waking reality. So, in dream space, a statue might weep or bleed. But on rare occasions such may occur in waking experience. So things normal only in dream space might now occur in waking space, such as levitation or bilocation or the odor of sanctity. The dream then is transformed into what appears to be physical reality. In view of the facts, our minds seem to have more power to mold physical reality than common experience suggests is possible.

An Irrepressible Yearning for the Miraculous

In our robust age of rationalism and terrorism, miracles may seem like comic interlopers; nevertheless, I believe that somewhere in our deep selves we yearn for them. The poet W.H. Auden said in *A Christmas Oratorio* that our mortality prompts us to "demand" a miracle. If Auden had said "beg for" or even "hope for," his line would be less poignant. But to *demand* a miracle is audacious and at the same time ironic.

During the 1990s, the notion was in the air that all manner of apocalyptic breakthroughs was at hand. But the new millennium arrived without cosmic ado. On the other hand, the 21st century seems a time in which the term *apocalyptic* is increasingly evoked. But this time science is proclaiming the dread news, not the prophets and old-time visionaries. Not everyone seems aware of what is going on, nevertheless a new consciousness is dawning that our species and all life on Earth are facing unprecedented dangers. A major overturning of world civilization is a theme that keeps gaining traction. This prospect is starting to reverberate in the collective psyche and is gaining a foothold in public consciousness. And yet endtime fantasies were always laced with promises of miraculous renewal. The prophets have always predicted the onset of the worst followed by supernatural rebirth. The classic millennium myth revolves around the thrilling idea of cosmic destruction and miraculous renewal.[17]

Miracles are woven into the great and small religions and philosophies. Miracles, we might say, are the agents of transcendence; they manifest in different ways in different times and cultures. The book of Exodus in the Hebrew bible is perhaps one of the all-time great miracle stories, beginning with Moses and his encounter with the burning bush (Exodus 3: 1-17) which was foundational for Judaism. Sufism is a psychospiritual branch into the mystical and miraculous dimension of Islam. Buddhism presents itself as a religion wed to its miracle lore, as Kenneth Woodward shows in his book on miracles. Here is the meaning of levitation in the context of Buddhism: "As a miraculous sign to the gods above that he has achieved enlightenment, the Buddha rises in the sky and declares his release from the karma-driven cycle of death and rebirth."[18]

Christianity is a religion rooted in the miracles of the Incarnation and the Resurrection. About Christianity, C.S. Lewis writes in his book *Miracles* (1947): "The mind which asks for a non-miraculous Christianity is a mind in process of relapsing from Christianity into mere 'religion.'" Lewis argues that Christianity is preeminently a miraculous religion. The reason is the Incarnation, the doctrine that God became a crucifiable man, and the Resurrection, the belief that a crucified man was raised from the dead.

These become major memes: first, God, in an act of friendliness toward humanity, becomes a human being and performs a divine drama on Earth in which he finally ascends back to Heaven, showing that we too may be crucified on Earth but can finally triumph in Heaven. That surely sounds encouraging. The second miracle is the good news that death can be transcended. It's hard to think of anything more personal. The Gospels overflow with miracle stories: healings, prophecies, exorcisms, walking on water, multiplication of food, reading of hearts, and so on. Meanwhile the man named Jesus astonishes the world with words and acts that show us what it means to be a human being inspired by the great spirit of radical love, the ultimate transformative miracle. Acts of the Apostles is a long miracle story, beginning with the day of Pentecost when the Holy Spirit descended on the disappointed disciples with a roar and in the form of tongues of fire that instantly forged a powerful group dynamic, turning them into driven apostles, thus launching the spread of what against all odds would spawn a new world religion. Something very strange and transformative happened on that day, (as it's said), the birthday of Christianity.

Miracles were rampant in the Middle Ages where God's presence and intervention in everyday life seemed commonplace. The world was a stage for miraculous displays.[19] Augustine said that the whole of creation and "all natural things are filled with the miraculous." For believers in a benevolent creator God, all things cast a miraculous sheen. "God himself has created all that is wonderful in this world, the great miracles as well as the minor marvels I have mentioned, and he has included them all in that unique wonder, that miracle of miracles, the world itself."[20]

The miraculous sense was strong during medieval times; the lives of the saints feature miracle stories recorded and evoked at their shrines. Every town had its shrine and miracle scribes. The relics of the saints and their burial places were occasions of miracles. A large medieval collection of miracle stories centered around Thomas Becket, the archbishop of Canterbury who was murdered in a cathedral in 1170. Miracles about avenging Becket's murder were proclaimed. Pilgrimages, a large part of medieval life, gave rise to miracle claims. Much miracle lore revolved around the Virgin, as in the legend of Saint Mary of Egypt, a converted prostitute whose unconfessed sins were miraculously revealed.

The strange and miraculous are found everywhere, beginning with descriptions of Australian aboriginal "men of high degree." Accounts of miraculous attainments or *siddhis* are a prominent part of Patanjali's classic *Yoga Sutras*. The Buddhist tradition, rooted in the level-headed realism of the founder's teachings, is nonetheless laden with miraculous tales, and the Islamic tradition is no less rich in the lore of holy marvels.

However retrograde belief in miracles may seem to some narrowly educated types today, there is no reason to believe that miracle claims will cease; in fact, they are more likely to proliferate during periods of violent disruption and transition. Despite the uneasy context, the world of miracles promises to take us to the outermost boundaries of the possible. Thomas Aquinas wrote: "The reason why the philosopher may be likened to the poet is this: both are concerned with the marvelous." In the preface to *Ecce Homo*, Nietzsche wrote that philosophy is "the search for all that is strange and questionable in existence" and in *Beyond Good and Evil* he defined the philosopher as one "who constantly experiences, sees, hears, suspects, and dreams extraordinary things." The philosophic impulse in us should therefore be cordial to miracle matters.

Do Such Beasts Really Exist?

The business of fact and evidence has to be approached concretely, on a case-by-case basis. We'll attempt to outline some *types* of paranormal provocation in a religious context from various sources. Stories, legends, but also sometimes eyewitness reports of miracles are found in Christian, Jewish, Hindu, Buddhist, Tibetan, Islamic, Chinese, and native shamanic and aboriginal traditions. Miracle stories belong to the heritage of all faiths and ethnicities. They're a universal part of human experience, and my wish is to probe their universal significance. Different cultures and belief-systems elicit different aspects of extraordinary human potential. I find myself asking whether the phenomena should be read as glimpses of what future humanity—if there is one—is likely to resemble. My answer to the question is that, yes, it's hard to resist wondering what the purpose of all strange phenomena might be—I mean more than just being entertaining flukes of nature. But let's have a look now at nature in some of its nonconformist, perverse, and contrarian moods.

Two: A Concise Anthology of Miracles

So, in a spirit of civic duty, I propose that we create a Miracle Park, a sanctuary for metaphysical outlaws to roam about in a spirit of freedom. The strangeness of the miracle animal is its intermundia status: in other words, miracles hover on the threshold betwixt and between the real and the surreal, fact and fiction, public and dream space, our ancient roots and our futuristic flowers. Whatever the power behind miracles, they appear like orphans of liminality, creatures of the threshold.

Why then bother with the curious but suspect world of miracles? One reason is to save them from the dogmatic clutches of religion; another to shield them from the repressive hand of science. Miracles, if the real deal, are something original in human experience. They suggest that great breakthroughs beyond the familiar habits of nature and our views of nature are possible. Miracles drive us to think outside the box of philosophical and scientific clichés. They force us to entertain the possibility of what we thought was impossible and to pay attention to what we do *not* know.

I'm drawn to the most extreme phenomena, as long as they're grounded in real testimony. Another point that needs to be made: sometimes miracle claims tally with empirical findings of psychical research and experimental parapsychology. This is helpful. We are trying to form a big picture. So, as far as I can see, scattered throughout human experience, there are signs, hints, and effects that periodically manifest this unmapped, largely hidden miracle potential. In trying to assemble a coherent view, what emerges is a picture of a new species of human being. Different pieces can be assembled into a picture of novelty. The various data seem like pointers to a new stage of human evolution. Careful and bold, let's have a look at some specifics.

Aboriginal and Other Miracles

The Australian anthropologist known as A.P. Elkin studied aboriginal miracle-makers, *karadji*, "men of high degree," and described their abilities, including thought-transference, clairvoyance, immunity to fire, the power of disappearance, "fast travelling," and the ability to "create illusions."[21] Physicist Gary Holz, suffering from multiple sclerosis, travelled to the Australian Outback, and was healed by aboriginal shamans.[22] This is a story of a man who went against the advice of friends and family, and subjected himself to a painful process of emotional and cognitive transformation, with the striking result that he himself was transformed into a healer.

The fast traveling, or super-agility, of aboriginals is also reported of Tibetan yogis and Catholic saints like Magdalene de'Pazzi. The Belgian–French explorer and spiritualist Alexandra David-Neel observed entranced Tibetans walking at preternatural speeds, said to continue for 24 hours at a stretch. This and other extraordinary phenomena result from the practice of *lung-gom*, based on concentration of mind and breath-control. "According to Tibetans," writes David-Neel, "the body of those who drill themselves for years, by that method (*lung-gom*), become exceedingly light; nearly without weight. In fact, the aim is levitation."[23] The mystic saint Joseph of Copertino had other methods that led to his spectacular career of ecstatic levitation. Joseph became exceedingly light by fasting, lacerating his body, sublimating relentless sexual temptation, and above all by keeping his mind and heart fixed on the idea of heaven and the denizens of heaven whom he adored, such as the Madonna. The Madonna was the most frequent cause of the friar's anti-gravitational capers. A glance at her image in a painting or the sight of her statue or the sound of her name in a song, and Joseph would emit his usual wild scream and take to the air.

Supernormal rapidity of movement and levitation blend imperceptibly with another supernormal phenomenon—bilocation. Bilocation is a kind of absolute limit of fast walking; the person appears located in two distinct regions of physical space. No less strange, Alexandra David-Neel reports learning from her Tibetan miracle maestros how to create a spatially extended "thought form," in her case, a three-dimensional creature in the shape of a grungy leering man that acquired a life of his own, and which turned out to be a nuisance not easy to dispose of. These creatures are called *tulpas*, animated thought-forms. If such are for real, one wonders how many people we see passing in streets or shopping malls are tulpas or maybe ghosts; remember, not all ghosts are transparent or filmy like the one that once attacked me in a haunted house in New Jersey.[24] I'm afraid it's not possible to rule out the possibility that some of the people we meet in everyday life may be ghosts or tulpas.

I was once in the vestry of San Giovanni Rotundo, in Italy, talking with Father Bill Martin, the Brooklyn monk who shared with me tales of Padre Pio whom he fed in his last years. Father Martin stopped suddenly, and looked around. "You know," he said, waving his hand, "you can't be sure about the people you see walking through here—you never know if they're flesh or spirits." When he walked through the vestry with Padre Pio, the Padre would occasionally stop, fix his attention on some portion of empty space, and listen attentively. He might then say something like, "Go back" or "Not yet."

Studies of the anthropology and folklore of religion by the Scottish poet Andrew Lang contain keen observations on the paranormal kernels of religious life.[25] Lang was chagrined by scholars who ignored the paranormal in their study of religion. An anthropologist from the University of Virginia had the courage to record observations of preternatural phenomena; David Barker did field work with Tibetan refugees in Nepal in the early 1970s. Barker noted that Tibetans have no words for miracle or paranormal but see such things as natural byproducts of spiritual training, of achieving highly concentrated states of mind, as taught in Patanjali's *Yoga Sutras* and techniques of meditation. According to Barker, Tibetan spirituality understands "the world to be primarily psychokinetic, the creation of form by consciousness."[26] Weather control in Tibet is offered as proof of the commonly held belief in the psychokinetic nature of the world.

Barker observed an example of this in Dharamsala, India, on March 10, 1973. Gunsang Rinzing, a revered shaman, was asked by the Dalai Lama to stop a boisterous storm that was interfering with a festival of mourning for the 1959 destruction of the Tibetan state. The evening before the festival, the shaman built a fire during the downpour and with great concentration began to recite a mantra. By morning the rain was down to a drizzle and then turned into a cold fog over a circle covering a radius of about 150 meters. Several thousand refugees had gathered for the festival. Huge clattering hailstones kept falling on the adjoining grounds and everywhere *outside* the circle the downpour continued. The shaman had tended his fire and chanted for 20 hours straight; after the rite of mourning was complete, he was applauded for his performance. "The atmosphere at the grounds seemed to have an 'airless' quality," wrote Barker, "and the whole experience produced in me a feeling of distress and disorientation that persisted for weeks."

Christian Wonder Workers

The Christian tradition is a rich source of miracle data. A certain part is romance, fantasy, legend, and ideology. But the practice of deposing evidence for heroic sanctity and supernatural phenomena gradually led to massing eyewitness testimony to all manner of strange human behaviors. In the Catholic church, Vatican depositions from canonization processes, biographies of saints, scholarly studies of the Bollandists, and contemporary research contain narratives that attest to the existence of charisms, supernatural graces, and miracles.[27]

Many saintly phenomena seem to defy known physical law. Catholic historian Herbert Thurston began his study of the evidence for levitation by noting that although the saints have no monopoly on marvels, "the mighty works which they perform by the power of the

Most High are in every way more stupendous than the prodigies of natural and diabolical magic with which they are placed as it were in competition."[28] So, if the anomaly is not of Catholic provenance, it must be inferior in scope, merely magical or frankly diabolical? That is obviously presumptuous overreach.

However, Thurston is right in citing the Catholic mystics for their extraordinary phenomena. The highly critical Thurston singled out the case of Joseph of Copertino to illustrate the phenomenon of levitation. The legalistic Roman Church collects and assesses the evidence of its miracle-performing servants and has been at it for two thousand years. Miracles are part of the process that canonizes saints and are therefore integral to church identity.

Good evidence is relatively easy to provide for some phenomena. For example, consider levitation: you don't have to be a quantum physicist to correctly observe that a person has been lifted off the ground without any apparent mechanical cause. To judge whether somebody has been miraculously cured of cancer is far more difficult. One can doubt whether a diagnosis of cancer was mistaken; whether somebody was lifted off the ground is easily determined, barring organized duplicity or stage magic. All that is required is normal eyesight and the ability to describe what one has seen.

The Flying Monk

Credible witnesses observed Joseph of Copertino's surprisingly frequent levitations. Prosper Lambertini (later Pope Benedict XIV), a famously critical devil's advocate in Joseph's canonization process, stated that "eye-witnesses of unexceptionable character reported on the celebrated levitations and remarkable flights of this servant of God when in a condition of ecstatic rapture."[29] Joseph was so disposed to sudden trance and ecstatic states that he seemed in many ways unfit for a priestly vocation. His first efforts at entering religious life were not successful.

Jospeh was dismissed from several religious orders for being clumsy and intellectually handicapped; by a fluke he made it to the priesthood in 1628, his final exam waived because all the previous candidates passed with flying colors. So, not a good scholar or pious scribe, but in his will to strip himself bare of all vestiges of earth-bound humanity, and fling himself into the arms and bosom of the divine, he was a relentless practitioner.

Joseph fasted and tortured himself with hairshirt, chains, and other contraptions he tied to his body. By no means graceful or discreet, his ecstasies caused so much disturbance that he was ejected from the choir and not allowed to eat in the rectory with his brothers. In spite of being a klutz and a nuisance and hauled before the Inquisition three times, Joseph's fame as mighty mystic, healer, precognizer, and levitator kept growing. On one occasion, the nuns of St. Ligorio observed him deep in prayer; suddenly, he gave his characteristic shriek and flew across the chapel to a crucifix mounted high on the altar. Afloat in a dream of ecstasy, he reached out and touched the figure on the cross. Beneath him lay tall vases of fresh flowers and a mini-forest of burning candles. The nuns were shocked and cried out: "He will catch fire! He will catch fire!"

Brother Lodovico, who was present and knew Joseph, explained to the nuns that the monk was a frequent flier and was immune to heat and flame. The depositions say that he gave forth with his famous cry and flew back to his place in the chapel where he proceeded to dance, whirl, and sing, exclaiming with joy and exultation: "Oh, most Blessed Virgin! oh most Blessed Virgin!" The Madonna was a powerful prompter of Joseph's airborne spiritual orgies. But in truth almost anything could prompt a flight. A casual word about God's beautiful sky might send him aloft.

The frequency, velocity, and duration of Joseph's raptures were observed and recorded over a period of 35 years. According to Pastrovicchi's 1753 biography, the acts of his beatification record 70 flights just for the period he resided in Copertino. Bystanders often reacted with unvarnished terror at the sight of the soaring friar. At times during Mass Joseph remained suspended in the air for two hours at a stretch. Witnesses were not just rubes but popes, princes, admirals, and ambassadors from all parts of Europe who came to witness the flying friar.

Note the immediate causes of his gravitational suspensions. In every instance, they are psychological, typically, ecstatic states. Alterations of mental state somehow enabled Joseph to escape the constraints of gravitation. Once he was ordered to kiss the feet of Pope Urban VIII; so awed, he flew to the ceiling and floated in rapture until he was called to his senses by the Father-General. In 1645, the Spanish Ambassador to the Papal Court and Admiral of Castile visited Assisi to see Joseph. The Ambassador arrived with his curious wife. "Scarcely had he (Joseph) entered the church when, looking up to a statue of the Immaculate Conception on the altar, he flew about twelve paces over the heads of those present to the foot of the statue. After remaining there for some time in prayer, he flew back with his customary cry and returned to his cell."[30]

The eyewitness testimony to his aerial capers is abundant and the Vatican archives contain about 150 different cases of sworn written testimony to his flights. In fact, the friar was known for these ecstasies and flights for 35 continuous years, often unpredictably in public, so thousands must have witnessed his levitations. This superphysical disregard of the most basic character of physical reality, gravity, is a large gauntlet thrown down before the scientific imagination. How can a peculiar state of mind disable the effects of gravity? How to account for the causal link between ecstasy and levitation?[31]

Levitation Viewed from Within

In her autobiography, St. Teresa of Avila talks about how it felt to levitate. "It comes, in general, as a shock, quick and sharp, before you can collect your thoughts, or help yourself in any way, and you see and feel it as a cloud, or a strong eagle rising upwards and carrying you away on its wings."[32] The great Carmelite nun and mystic describes her fear of this rapture and resistance to its onset: "I had no power over it—and now and then the whole body as well, so that it lifted me up from the ground." Lest you wonder whether Teresa was deluded, eyewitness testimony backs up her claims. Sister Anne of the Incarnation at Segovia deposed under oath that at two o'clock in broad daylight she observed Teresa enter the choir and kneel down: "As I was looking on, she was raised about half a yard from the ground without her feet touching it. At this I was terrified and she, for her part, was trembling all over. So I moved to where she was and I put my hands under her feet, over which I remained weeping for something like half an hour while the ecstasy lasted."[33]

Thurston provides detailed examples of levitation and asserts that about 200 cases could be invoked to confirm the reality of these mind-bending phenomena. Also famous in the world of levitators is the Victorian medium, D.D. Home, who was observed to levitate on many occasions, and was investigated by one of the leading physicists of his day, Sir William Crookes. Other physical mediums like Eusapia Palladino were famous for levitating physical objects like tables.[34] It seems the phenomenon depends on a radically altered state of mind in which one's normal sense of identity is temporarily but completely dissolved. Levitation appears to be a physical manifestation of a special, detached state of mind. There is a continuum of effects that border on levitation; for example, reports of a featherlike, super-agility in the behavior of Saint Mary Magdalena de' Pazzi.[35] Lightening up may be a mental state that can directly affect physical reality. In time what first seemed impossible will come to seem inevitable, and the point will come when we realize there may not be any limits to our possible physical influence.

The Stigmatist as Performance Artist

However we decide to interpret the stigmata, as a product of hysteria or a divine sign, the replication of the wounds of Christ are highly *expressive* artifacts. In that sense, they're like works of performance art. But something else of interest may be involved; stigmata may shed light on human evolution, suggested Ian Wilson in his 1989 study of the phenomenon.[36] Stigmata are reminders of the plasticity of the body and the power of a willful imagination. It has implications for psychosomatic medicine, as well possibly for the concept of evolution. Anything that proves such malleability of the body to mental influence is also saying something about the causal role of mind in health and disease.

Saint Francis of Assisi is the first well-known case and became the exemplar others have echoed for centuries. Soon after his death, Brother Elias sent a letter to the Provincial of France: "I announce to you great joy," he wrote, "even a new miracle."[37] The new miracle were the stigmata. The eyewitness account of Thomas of Celano states: "Now these marks were found on the inner side of the hands and elongated on the outer, and certain small pieces of flesh were seen like the ends of nails bent and driven back, projecting from the rest of the flesh." The same thing was observed on the feet. The nail heads, moreover, that formed out of his flesh became black like the color of iron. Says Thurston: "No power of autosuggestion, no abnormal pathological conditions could enable a contemplative to evolve from the flesh of his hands and feet four horny excrescences in the form of nails piercing his extremities."

Thurston concludes that this transformation was "miraculous," and that it forces us to admit God's intervention. That of course is Thurston's faith speaking, but there is no doubt that what happened to the body of Francis of Assisi was very strange indeed. But then we do know that women experience pseudocyesis; that is, they produce all the physical symptoms of pregnancy, which fool their doctors, but they are not actually pregnant.

This seems to show that under certain conditions the body may attain expressive power that transcends its customary physiological capacities and presumed genetic potentials. The stigmata of Francis of Assisi we could say were the result of highly expressive endosomatic psychokinesis. It may have also involved an external transpersonal influence. This phenomenon seems to fit the ancient Platonic conception of the body as an "instrument of the soul." It blatantly counters reductive materialism that would forbid such a relationship, according to which the mental must be without causal power or existence. The stigmata of Francis of Assisi flatly contradict that.

Since the 13th century roughly 400 cases of stigmata have been recorded, the majority being women in Catholic countries. I view stigmatists as performance artists because their wounds, which replicate the wounds of the crucified Christ, are meant to re-enact an archetype of the Christian faith. They are often performed in public on Good Friday or other symbolic times commemorating the crucifixion.

Padre Pio said Mass for 50 years using hands covered with blood-soaked mittens to raise the consecrated chalice and perform the rite in full view of packed church audiences. It certainly appears that intense identification with and concentration upon the image of the crucified savior had *something* to do with producing the phenomenon, despite the fact that the Padre himself once made fun of such an idea.

As with levitation, stigmata seem like spectacular demonstrations of directed interior states that can modify known physical "laws" and mold them in accord with a powerfully focused intention. One wonders what might happen if Christians focused more on the resurrection body of Christ instead of the crucified body. There might well be an increase in reports of ecstatic levitation. Imagination oriented toward the belief in the resurrection might generate optimal physical states.

The surprising saintly effects resonate with other known psychological phenomena, related, for example, to hypnotic effects. In one notable case, a patient suffering from congenital ichthyosis (fish-skin disease) was largely cured by hypnotic treatment. One can imagine an alternate history of Christianity that featured identification with the resurrected instead of the crucified body. Why the manipulative fixation on being nailed to a cross? The German poet Heinrich Heine wrote disparagingly of what he deemed the morbid obsession with a crucified god. It is at least conceivable that a new phase of historic Christianity will yet unfold in tune with a more optimal vision of embodied life.

The stigmata demonstrate the evolutionary power of the body to mutate into something that conforms to the interests of the spiritual imagination. Stigmata occur in response to visions or artistic representations of the crucifixion. With growing historical knowledge and attention to the Shroud of Turin, the view now is that the Romans crucified their victims through the wrists.

The inspiration for most stigmatists seems to have been the artistic representation of the crucifixion, not the historical reality. The stigmata have in part been a case of reality imitating art; they seem more like miracles of the mimetic imagination than replications of the historical crucifixion. Also, as in many cases (for example, Therese Neumann), the stigmata appear temporarily during Good Friday, a fact that also suggests the mimetic imagination at work.

Padre Pio's stigmata are perhaps the most carefully studied and in some ways the most puzzling on record. For one thing, it is hard to explain them as the product of hysterical personality. No credible evidence exists proving him to be mentally unhinged the way records show stigmatists such as Louise Lateau clearly were. His wounds were continuously manifest for 50 years but never became infected. The blood reportedly produced various fragrances, a part of the saintly miracle syndrome. Without a shred of evidence, early detractors accused the Padre of being a dandy, a secret user of exotic perfumes. Toward the time of his death the wounds gradually healed, and at his death the last scales fell from them, leaving no sign of scarred tissue. Could an open wound of five decades spontaneously heal *and leave no scar*? I asked Dr. Eugene Sweeny, a Columbia University dermatologist. He said such a thing was completely outside his experience.

Rings of Mystical Love

One of the less discussed miracles involve "tokens of espousal." They are found in the lives of saintly women who believe themselves mystically espoused to Christ; a kind of marriage ring appears on the betrothed's finger. In 1367, St. Catherine of Siena had a vision of being espoused to Christ, in which the Madonna herself placed a wedding ring on her finger. Catherine confessed to her biographer,

Raymond of Capua, that from that day on, the ring remained visible on her finger—though invisible to everyone else. The skeptic will of course smile. An invisible ring? Catherine's ring-finger was kept as a relic by the Carthusians of Pontignano. Question: what does it take to produce a *permanent* hallucination? Hallucinations are brief; some apparently go on and on. Another possibility is that Catherine was just lying, but there are no reasons to suggest she was consciously fabricating a tale.

Rings of espousal go a step further in baffling our expectations of what nature can produce. Marie-Julie Jahenny had the stigmata, and during one of her ecstatic wanderings, announced her mystical espousal to the heavenly Son. Witnesses should be present on February 20, 1874, for a ring of espousal to Jesus was going to appear on her finger. The Bishop arranged for 14 witnesses to be present with Marie-Julie on that day. One of the eyewitnesses wrote to Dr. Imbert-Gourbeyre: "At nine o'clock all the wounds (stigmata) began to bleed. At a quarter past we perceived that the finger was becoming swollen and reddening under the skin. At about quarter to ten blood was running from the upper and lower surface of the finger, and by degrees we saw the ring take shape. It is now clearly marked for all her life to come." In 1894, Imbert-Gourbeyre wrote: "Marie-Julie's ring remains to the present day. I saw it again in October, 1891, still a ring made of the fleshy tissues, like a hoop of red coral which had sunk into the skin."[38]

This phenomenon seems beyond the pale of psychosomatic medicine. Embarrassment or rage might send blood to the head and cause one to blush. But that a vision could cause blood and epidermis to assume the form of a ring on a finger is off the chart of what we would normally entertain is possible. Once again it appears that in certain circumstances the imagination possesses extraordinary creative power over the body.

As for Marie-Julie's predicting the exact time her nuptial ring would appear, many accounts are available of saints, yogis, and Zen masters predicting the exact time of their death. An unconscious time mechanism may come into play in more sinister fashion when stigmatists, identifying with Christ's crucifixion, die at the age of 33, as happened with St. Catherine of Siena, Louise Lateau, Madeleine Morise, Teresa Musco, Mother Agnes of Jesus, Domenica Lazzari, and others. Expectation can be a powerful agent of transformation.

Sometimes the unconscious suggestion of death is planted by someone else. I have a written account from a nurse telling the story of her husband's demise. He was a young man when he visited a fortune teller in New Orleans. The fortune teller said he was going to have a wonderful life until the age of 35, at which time he would die. When he reached that age, he became ill and died; an autopsy, according to the nurse who had access to the medical records, revealed no known cause of death. He had told his wife he was sensing the onset of death; his wife reassured him he had nothing to worry about, he was fine, but she was wrong. His imagination destroyed him.

Back to rings of espousal. Here is a description from a Sister Mary who observed St. Veronica Giuliani's ring: "It encircled her ring-finger exactly as ordinary rings do. On the outside there appeared to be a raised stone, as large as a pea, and of a red color…" As with Thomas of Celano's account of the stigmata of Saint Francis, where a hard nail-shaped protuberance appeared, here is another example of a transformation of living flesh under the influence of an idea. Ideas, not just material forces and structures, can in principle shape our embodied lives. The stigmata and rings of espousal are vivid illustrations of this potential.

The Telekinetic Host

Catholic hagiography is full of stories of willful, gravity-perverse Eucharistic Hosts. Raymond of Capua encountered this several times with Catherine of Siena: "The thought had hardly framed itself in my mind, before I touched It, the Sacred Host, as I clearly perceived, moved forward of Itself, the distance of three inches or more, coming close to the paten which I was holding in my hand."[39] Here the impatience of the communicant is imparted to the inert material host.

Stigmata, rings of espousal, Sacred Hosts, and much more in the lore of Catholic mysticism are rich in symbolic significance and figure in reports of miraculous happenings. Many of the phenomena called "miracles" involve objects charged with sacred meaning. Rings of espousal speak to the need for intimate communion, as the stigmata speak to the willingness to endure the pains of crucifixion for the sake of sacred power. The telekinetic host reflects a kind of superhuman impatience for divine infusion.

Mystical Torches

In the world of miracles, metaphors have a way of coming to life in strange ways. For example, in the biography of St. Lidwina of Schiedam, written by Thomas á Kempis, we read: "And although she always lay in darkness and material light was unbearable to her eyes, the divine light was very agreeable to her, and her cell was often so wonderfully flooded by light that it appeared full of material lamps and fires."

So in this case again the inner seems to objectify itself as something outer. Subjectivity, in accord with the degree of its intensity, tends to materialize and objectify. The enlightened state of the spiritual seeker becomes visible, turns into an atmosphere of light; the boundary between inner and outer seems to dissolve. In Iranian Sufism, Henry Corbin's *The Man of Light* (1971) is an account of a mystical tradition oriented around light, color, along with painting as sacred calligraphy. Light and color are part of the language of the soul we need to learn and represent a new range of research that connects imaginative art to the project of human evolution.

The Odor of Sanctity

Another example of a sense raised to mystical heights is the sense of smell, as is often said of the odor of sanctity. In this well-known phenomenon, persons of inner quality and purity in various ways reveal transcendent fragrances. The best illustration I know of may be found in "The Miraculous Odor of Virginity," a chapter in the biography (*Wings of Ecstasy*, 2017) of the great flying mystic, Joseph of Copertino, which provides numerous sworn testimonials to the reality of Joseph's paranormal olfactions. The surgeon F. Pierpaoli, who did an autopsy on him, spoke of the "perfume that always emanated from his body." His cell continued to emanate this perfume for 12 or 13 years after his death.

Giovanni Maria deposed: "That perfume spread through all the cells and lingered on in clothes which, though washed often with soap and lye, never lose the fragrance." Cardinal Giulio Spinola wrote under oath: "When I entered that little cell, the sweetest perfume would cheer me up and I could compare it to nothing in nature or in the art of man. . . .the perfume of Padre Giuseppe brought me the greatest pleasure and seemed even to heal my body." This strange phenomenon is said to have been a product of Joseph's lifelong virginity, a state of affairs that Bernini reminds us Joseph had to struggle very hard to maintain. It is certainly a surprising fact that prolonged sublimation of sexual desire should somehow create such a transcendent perfume.

The bodily remains and relics of saintly folk reportedly occasion various olfactory marvels. Saint Teresa was famous for her otherworldly odor, and Saint Veronica of Giuliani's stigmata—like Padre Pio's—suffused unnatural fragrances. Strange fragrances haunt the tombs and relics of dead saints. The message seems clear enough and would have us dissociate death from the stench of decay. Instead, it wants us to associate the smells of springtime with the normally depressing idea of death, and all this in complete defiance of commonsense. I have to ask: where is this "miracle" coming from? The trickster, the subconscious fabricator of myth? Or is it a graphic message from a transcendent world of conscious intentionality?

Immunity to Fire

Now consider another indicator of a capacity to change our relationship to nature. Some individuals in certain circumstances may become exempt from the normal effects of heat and fire; also, some people have uncanny capacities to generate heat from their bodies.

Together, we may speak of mastery of fire. In chapter 3 of the Book of Daniel, we read the story of three youths, Hanania, Mishael, and Azaria, (their Babylonian names were Shadrach, Meshach, and Abednego); they refused to bow before an image of the King of Babylon, so were thrown into a fiery furnace. When Nebuchadnezzar saw the lads walking unharmed in the fire, he yanked them out of the furnace and offered them positions in high office, with the added perk of decreeing that anyone harming the fire-transcending performers would be torn limb from limb. This is not the only story about higher powers seeming to intervene to alleviate existential threat and even come to the rescue of justice.

A salamander is a mythical creature said to be immune to fire. In line with the story in the Book of Daniel, the records of some extremists in holiness may appear like human salamanders. According to sworn testimony, Saint Francis of Paula was immune to the effects of fire. One witness deposed that the Saint picked up a large piece of red-hot iron; when someone shouted he'd be burnt, Francis replied: "By your leave, I am just holding it to warm myself." A joker, as well as a miracle man.

It is said that he once put his arm in a kettle of boiling oil, another time in boiling lye. A Bishop sent to test his avowed saintliness said: "It's easy for you to touch fire because you're a peasant." Francis stooped down and picked up a few red-hot coals and burning brands in his bare hands. Holding them casually, he turned to the Canon and said with genial mockery: "You see, I couldn't do this, if I weren't a peasant."

Supernormal talents like immunity to fire can temporarily be transmitted to others by a kind of psycho-energetic contagion. And here we have indications of the miraculous potential of certain kinds of group consciousness. Thurston points out that St. Francis of Paula often handed live coals and burning brands to people without saying much, casually testing their faith. Confortus de Affriento saw that a fired lime-kiln needed to be fixed, but the door to the kiln was so small it was hard for a grown man to enter. So Francis of Paula invited a brother who was notably small to squeeze through the small door and do the job. He did so and emerged unburned and unhurt.

There is good eyewitness testimony of incombustibility in the case of the physical medium Daniel Dunglas Home. In 1869, Lord Lindsay deposed his testimony for the Committee of the Dialectical Society: "I have frequently seen Home, when in a trance, go to the fire and take out large red-hot coals, and carry them about in his hands, put them inside his shirt, and so on. Eight times I have myself held a red-hot coal in my hands without injury, though it scorched my face on raising my hand."[40] Home was not especially holy or unworldly; his gifts matured and manifested in a social context of class, science, the churches, the press, but he displayed abilities often enough associated with saintly religiosity.

Again, an indication that (what we are calling) miracles are not the property of one group or type of individual. Rather, I believe they are waiting to happen, ready when the right conditions for manifestation come together. Sometimes the capacity—if that's the right word—is achieved by contagion. Lord Lindsay acquired temporary immunity to fire in the presence of D.D. Home. A saint or medium can draw a rightly disposed person into a psychic circle where impossible behaviors temporarily become actual.

Firewalking ceremonies practiced around the world today exhibit various degrees of immunity to fire, as sociologist James McClenon explains.[41] McClenon himself rather bravely tried firewalking eight times, going back to master it after suffering a blistering mishap during his second experiment. According to McClenon, firewalking is used in some cultures to enhance self-esteem and to activate the power of the placebo effect—ideas worthy of further exploration.

Support for McClenon's claims on the life-enhancing powers of fire-walking comes from *Extreme Spirituality*, a book by Tolly Burkan. In the foreword, Andrew Weil, the American physician, described his own fire-walking experiments. Weil walked barefoot over a bed of hot glowing coals three times. Twice he felt pain and injured himself; the third time, he slipped into the right state of mind and walked over the coals without pain or injury.[42] Finally, I should add that the mythologist Joseph Campbell once told me of his success in a firewalking ceremony, on a day we met crossing Sixth Avenue in Greenwich Village, New York.

Bodily Elongation

Many of the marvels of the saints are matched by similar marvels of mediums. For example, the unedifying miracle of bodily elongation, where a person is *measured* and found to be temporarily elongated like Alice was elongated in Wonderland, or like a figure in an El Greco painting. Lord Adare, an English aristocrat charmed by D.D. Home's strange talents, wrote of the medium's April 3, 1869, elongation: "While his arms appeared to be increasing in length, his chest became greatly expanded, and he said to me: 'You see how it is; the extension is from the chest.' He then placed himself against the wall, and extended his arms to their full natural length; I made a pencil mark at the tip of his fingers. His left arm was then elongated. . . . The total elongation, as ascertained by this means, amounted to nine and one half inches."[43]A stunning assertion, as it is hard to suppose that Lord Adare made a *nine and one half* inch mistake in measuring Home's arm.

Bodily elongation is not in the least edifying or useful; rather, it repulsed and frightened witnesses, which is a reason for doubting it was an invented tale. Thurston doesn't quite know what to make of this odd phenomenon except to say it usually occurred to a person who was in a trance state. To my mind, saintly elongation is comically reminiscent of cartoons, caricatures, and expressionistic painting; it hints of the humorous, the "smiling" side of the miraculous, and another sign of bodily plasticity, another way of mocking the idea of mechanical models of embodied existence.

Symbolic Miracles

A metaphor we meet in the annals of sainthood is the *ardor of love*. This term is used by mystics to denote the expression of spiritual ardor in the form of fire, heat, and scintilla, expressing the physical heat of divine passion, which we may plausibly link with the erotic. With Catherine of Genoa, the heat of mystical passion was so intense that when "a large silver cup was ordered to be brought in, which had a very high standing saucer; the cup was full of cold water for refreshing her hands, in the palms of which, because of the great fire that burned within her, she felt intolerable pain. And on putting her hands into it, the water became so boiling that the cup and the very saucer were greatly heated."[44] In all ways this lady was truly *hot*.

Hagiography is rife with tales of *incendium amoris*—"the fire of love." Here is one from the biography of the Venerable Serafino di Dio, a Carmelite nun who died in 1699. From her beatification process: "The nuns say that they have often seen her—for example, when she was in prayer, or after Communion—with her face glowing like a flame and her eyes sparkling. It scorched them if they touched her, even in winter time and even when she was quite old, and they declared that they had repeatedly heard her say that she was consumed with a living fire and that her blood was boiling."[45] Inner ardor becomes physical flame, symbolic longing turns into mind-stopping events in public space. It seems like a development we could do without on our overheated planet.

Inedia, the Miraculous Diet

Many reported miracles revolve around basic physical sensations: weight, light, heat, and smell. Some are around eating. Eating is a basic fact of organic life, yet the Hebrew sage says that man lives not by bread alone. Christian faith is built around the Eucharist rite, in which the celebrant ingests the divine wafer, introducing the idea of supernatural nutrition. Many saints were known for their prodigious fasts that on their face were *super*-natural. Extensive fasting is associated with charisms, a term for supernatural gifts. Why fasting? Anything, in fact, that disrupts the routine rhythms of sensori-motor life might lower the threshold of awareness and thus increase receptivity to psychic impressions. Fasting is an ancient method for inducing altered states of awareness more receptive to fringe regions of experience.

On a visit to San Giovanni Rotundo, Foggia, in 1986, I spoke about Padre Pio's eating habits with Father Bill Martin, who had been assigned the task of feeding the Padre in the last years of his life. I was not surprised to learn that Padre Pio ate almost nothing, and in light of his daily loss of blood and poor health, it was a miracle that he managed to survive at all, let alone fend off the thousands of pilgrims that besieged him daily.

Apparently, there are people who live for prolonged periods with little or no food or drink, and in some cases, without that sure sign of nature, elimination. Inediacs, people who live without eating like Louise Lateau or Mollie Fancher, are often bed-ridden and afflicted with numerous health issues. But the most famous inediac of the 20th century was quite robust and normal, apart from her supernormal and highly dramatic talents. Therese Neumann, a Bavarian Catholic who lived through the Nazi era, was a visionary who displayed the stigmata. That seems to have been their *raison d'etre*: to display the idea of the crucifixion. Her wounds became visible exclusively on Thursdays and Fridays when she would exude much blood, sometimes through her eyes, surely one of the ghastliest of "charisms."

Because of a muscle spasm in her throat in 1922, she stopped eating solid food; by 1926 all she could manage was to drink a few drops of water. On August 6, 1926, she had a vision of Christ's Transfiguration, and hunger and thirst permanently left her. By 1927 she quit all forms of nourishment, except a daily eighth of a communion wafer. She stopped eliminating, and continued in this state for the remaining 35 years of her life, according to the official account.[46]

Exceptionally, she was not bed-ridden but healthy, energetic, and robust. She lived very much a public life, made herself accessible to visitors, and was fond of nature and sightseeing excursions. Friends, family, and religious confessors never saw her eat despite spending hours working with her in the fields or going on outings with her that lasted for days. Her brother said that despite the heat she never drank or showed signs of fatigue. Witnesses swore to all this under oath, and there are no grounds I am acquainted with that suggest they conspired to mislead the public or were driven by unconscious forces to fabricate their story.

Naturally, one wonders whether Therese ate or drank on the sly. To make sure this was not the case, and in response to widespread requests to test her, she consented to being observed in July 1927 by a medical commission and four Mallersdorf nurses whose veracity was placed under oath. She was intimately probed and carefully observed for 15 continuous days and nights. At all times she was under observation by at least two nurses. Powerful arc lamps beamed 5000 watts in her eyes to test the authenticity of her ecstasies (she showed no reactions). She lost about eight pounds after her stigmata bled but by the end of the experiment her weight was somehow restored.

Only by assuming a wildly improbable conspiracy can you doubt the conclusion: for more than two weeks she drank and ate nothing but tiny shards of the Eucharist wafer. So well-known was her inediac lifestyle that during the war the Third Reich gave her no food rations. When asked how she managed, she replied that she was nourished by the Light of her Savior.

In *Autobiography of a Yogi*, Yogananda tells the story of a Hindu woman named Giri Bala. Yogananda heard of this woman and tracked her down in Northern Bengal where she declared to him that she had ceased eating and drinking 58 years ago. The Maharaja of Burdwan had locked her up in his palace on three occasions, once for two months, to test Giri Bala's inedia and had concluded that she was the real deal. Unfortunately, we have no documented evidence in support of this intriguing story, which has parallels in the Catholic tradition. The Hindu holy woman claimed to nourish herself on air and sunlight; the Catholic inediac claims to be nourished by God and the minute scraps of the Eucharistic host, which is thought to be a morsel of God materialized.

Divine Short Order Cooks

Let's then assume for a moment the reality of inedia and that it is possible to live on (so to speak) spirit alone; in that case, it might also be possible to create or at least teleport food around. Jesus is supposed to have done it, and there are stories of Mohammed performing this miracle, of Sai Baba in modern times materializing hot lunches, and of Christian saints providing food for the hungry in strange ways. And let's not forget the manna that fell from heaven to nourish the Israelites. Manna, bread from Heaven, according to the Bible, was the food that fed the Israelites for 40 years of wandering in the wilderness (Ex. 16-34).[47]

The food-manifesting marvels of Catholic saints worked like this. First of all, it was mainly in response to an urgent need, poverty, real hunger. Second, the food never quite appears out of nowhere; the miracle was always more beguiling. Large numbers of hungry and needy people would be fed from stores that were blatantly scant, but that somehow, slyly and surreptitiously, replenished themselves.[48] It was as if there were holes in the ill-stocked bottles, bowls, and cupboards, so when a small effort was made, a little groping in the corner or reaching down into a crevice, and the bread or piece of fish or extra wine would suddenly be there. E. Cobham Brewer's scholarly *A Dictionary of Miracles* (1884) gives many examples of food miracles, ranging from Elisha (Kings, 4:1-7) to St. Bridget.[49] The Christian prototype is the story of Jesus and the multiplication of loaves and fishes (Matt. 14:15-21).

Perhaps there is a larger lesson here about how it might be possible to experience need, a refusal to despair, a refusal to accept that every resource has been spent. Turning water into wine at the wedding in Cana (Jn.2: 1-12) signaled the debut of Jesus as wonder-worker. It's hard not to like this story. Instead of telling people to settle for water at a wedding party where the wine had run out, he chose to turn the water into wine! He could have said; let's keep a stiff puritanical lip and settle for plain water, and be consoled by the money we saved. But, as Baudelaire said, there are times when it's our duty to be drunken, and Jesus seems to have been of that mind, and respected the need for the spirit of festive disinhibition. No penny-pinching abstinence here, nothing Calvinistic; instead we are presented with a miracle that affirms the joys and virtues of the vine.

Nature in Service to Imagination

On May 26, 1907, in the small French town of Remiremont, a storm caused a sensation because the image of the Virgin Mary appeared engraved on hailstones that fell from the sky. Since 910 the town church housed a cedarwood statue of the Virgin Mary called Our Lady of the Treasure. The townsfolk believed the statue, originally a gift of Charlemagne, possessed supernatural power, and it was an annual custom to display it in a public procession. In 1682 the town was struck by an earthquake. The statue was brought out into the streets, and the aftershocks ceased. Our Lady of the Treasure thus acquired a reputation as miracle maker. Of course, it may have been a coincidence; it just didn't feel like a coincidence.

Then in 1907 the statue became the focus of a bitter controversy. Due to sectarian conflict within the Catholic establishment at Remiremont, the town council canceled the annual public ceremony in which Our Lady of the Treasure was to be crowned. A small but vocal anti-clerical faction had succeeded in suppressing a popular event honoring Our Lady. To compensate for this remiss, a medallion portraying the Virgin was struck. The day of the procession came and passed; and the edict against the crowning outraged the villagers.

On May 26th Remiremont was hit by some very wild weather. It had been a sunny day but by afternoon a storm rose from the southeast and for 45 minutes huge hailstones pelted the village. Something astonishing then happened. The townsfolk were amazed to discover that the outsized hailstones were impressed with an image of the Virgin that matched the image on the medallion of Our Lady that had been struck to honor her. Believers and skeptics alike inspected the hailstones, which were preserved for as long as possible.

One such skeptic was the Abbe Gueniot who wrote in 1908: "In order to satisfy her (a woman anxious for him to see what was happening), I glanced carelessly at the hailstones, which she held in her hand. But since I did not want to see anything, and moreover could not do so without my spectacles, I turned to go back to my book. She urged: 'I beg of you to put on your glasses.'" He continues, "I did so, and saw very distinctly on the front of the hailstones . . . the bust of a woman, with a robe that was turned up at the bottom, like a priest's cope." The report explains how the Abbe resisted looking at the details and how he felt ashamed of his credulity, but then adds: "But my mind was disturbed by the singular formation of these hailstones. . . . One of them was perfectly round, like balls with which children play, and had a seam all around it, as though it had been cast in a mold."[50]

There were two written reports of this phenomenon based on interviews with eyewitnesses, one by M.J. Vuillemin[51] and the other by M. Sage.[52] Abbe Vuillemin collected 107 depositions written under oath, stating that they saw the image of Our Lady of the Treasure on the hailstones. Vuillemin was conscious of the possibility of illusion and auto-suggestion but felt that the consistency and the details of the reported observations ruled that out. Observers reported that the images on the hailstones matched perfectly the images on their medallions, which reproduced the image of the statue of Our Lady of the Treasure.

Sage's report was negative but deficient on several counts. First, his interviews were conducted a year after Vuillemin's, and he was only able to obtain a dozen or so, largely because by that time the villagers had become mistrustful of outsiders. The local anti-clerical newspapers had attacked and ridiculed the townspeople as credulous and superstitious. Second, Sage's chief argument against authenticity seems to have been *ad hominem* and therefore fallacious; he insisted that the witnesses were uneducated peasants and that therefore their observations could not be trusted. But this reasoning is worthless, for peasants and farmers accustomed to pay attention to hailstorms are likely to be better observers than most city dwellers.

Journalist and researcher Scott Rogo reported that the behavior of the hailstones had features resembling poltergeists. For example, many witnesses described the descent of the large, imprinted hailstones as if they were guided in slow-motion by an invisible force. Also, the hailstones, despite falling on gardens, destroyed none of the vegetation. The slow-motion descent and selective non-destructiveness are features observed in poltergeist projectiles.

The miraculous hailstones may have been the product of collective frustration and hostility, the unconscious creation of people responding to threats against customs that had been a psychological mainstay for centuries. Rogo concludes: "Here we have what might be called a poltergeist potential being shared by the entire town. Its inhabitants were, in effect, manipulated into a psychological situation suspiciously similar to the one in which most poltergeist agents find themselves."[53] This model of collectively engendered miracles raises some startling possibilities. The next story might be another such example.

A Periodic Miracle with Group Dynamic

There is something ad hoc and improvisational about most miracles. But a few cases of periodic or recurrent miracles may be cited: for example, the acclaimed liquefaction of the blood of Saint Januarius, a Roman martyr, whom the Emperor Diocletian had beheaded at Pozzuoli in 305 (CE). Allegedly, the clotted blood of the saint is contained in a sealed glass vial, part of a silver reliquary. Like the statue of Our Lady of the Treasure in Remiremont, the reliquary of the saint's dried blood is placed on display several times a year in the Cathedral of Naples before excited throngs of pilgrims and believers.

The miracle? Apparently, the dried blood, sealed from the external world inside its glass reliquary, inexplicably *liquefies*. Liquefaction occurs immediately, in hours, or in days. The liquid mass appears to boil and froth, the color changes from dark brown to reddish brown, and the volume and weight reportedly increase. Re-clotting occurs when the vial is returned to a locked vault.

The phenomenon was mentioned for the first time in 1389 by a

Neapolitan chronicler. It is remarkable that this effect seems to occur on demand; the people pray and chant for it to happen, and it almost always does. But there is a confounding fact: the dried blood on occasion appears to liquefy on its own; movement of the vial may by itself suffice to start the liquefaction. Moreover, during the ceremony the reliquary is moved about.

So this miracle may have some problems. There may not be anything paranormal going on at all. First of all, it's not definitely known that the substance in the vial really is blood. The Catholic Church forbids opening the vial for direct examination. In 1902 a prism spectroscope was used to detect the presence of hemoglobin. A similar test was performed in 1989 with similar positive results. Members of the Italian Committee for the Investigation of Claims of the Paranormal assert that these tests were poorly conducted. Both, they say, used an old-fashioned spectroscope instead of a reliable modern electronic spectrophotometer.[54] The authors raise other objections to the tests, pointing out, for example, that red dyes in the substance might be mistaken for hemoglobin.

In addition, they offer a normal explanation of the liquefaction and re-clotting. Thixotropy refers to certain gels that alternately solidify and liquefy in response to shaking, stirring, or vibrating. Such gels were available to scientists and artists in 1389, a time when miraculous relics were in high demand. The thixotropic hypothesis seems to me a plausible explanation, but the chemists have yet to prove their case. If the substance in the vial turns out to be blood after all, their theory falls to pieces. Church authorities should allow scientists to use the best available technology to determine exactly what's inside the vial.

I do not know what the results will be. If there is no blood in the vial, it would suggest a brilliantly clever talent for hoaxing the pious imagination. Nevertheless, from a practical viewpoint, belief in the miracle of Saint Januarius has for centuries served as a powerful religious placebo. It would be hard to determine how it may have helped people in the past.

The miracle's imagery and symbolism are part of its value, the amphibious metaphysics of the solid and the liquid that the story seems to exemplify. The central image is that of liquefaction and ebullience. Is there a message about the need in a figurative, perhaps metaphysical, sense to *liquefy*? Are we too solid in the way we partition reality into I and not-I? Sacred and profane?

Apart from the insights of modern physics, we know from experience how unsolid the world really is. The solid citizen may be a terrorist; the solid business deal a ruthless scam; the solid relationship can dissolve in a minute. The Januarius miracle story may be telling us we're too rigid (too solid) about how we think of the real and the possible. I accept it as a request for cultivating a more fluid sense of reality.

The group dynamic of the liquefaction miracle is noteworthy. There is the crucial role of the *zie*, the "aunts" who summon the miracle, evoke it with their needy and pitiful cries. The women of the community station themselves in the cathedral and cry out for liquefaction; they wail for the miracle that Auden says we demand before we must die. Apart from what's really happening in the sacred vial, the story says something about the possibility of miraculous group dynamics. The Italian investigator Massimo Biondi has pointed out to me that there is a concentration of blood prodigies in Southern Italy and the cause may lie in the geo-magnetism of the region.[55] This may well be a factor that amplifies the process, but I'm inclined to think that paranormal group dynamics is the key to ultimate understanding.

There is a statement in Saint Matthew's gospel about the power of agreement: "Again I say unto you, that if two of you shall agree on earth as touching anything that they shall ask, it shall be done for them of my Father which is in heaven." That is an amazing promise and a statement about paranormal group dynamics. What does "agree" mean here? If we agree in our thoughts and feelings, if we harmonize our intentions—*symphonein* is the Greek word—if we psychically resonate, if we voice our minds in unison, we can ignite miracles.

English psychologist Kenneth Batcheldor and colleagues have experimented with paranormal group dynamics[56]and found that ordinary people in *the right group setting* could learn to levitate tables without contact. A paradigm-busting claim, one is inclined to say. If miracles do occur, they often enough do seem to be effects of a special group dynamic. The experience at Pentecost of visitation via tongues of flame was a group event with a powerful story and a dynamic that took off in history. As another example of paranormal group dynamics, let's glance backward to ancient Greece, to a very different kind of group dynamic.

Dionysos, Miracles, and Madwomen

Cultures create rites and myths that more or less favor the occurrence of miracles. The cult of Dionysos is an example, an outlier at odds with the serene rationality we associate with classical Greece. Dionysos (the god) was a disturbing oddball in the eyes of the Olympian deities. The cult, the religion, the manic energy took root in the 8th century BCE and spread to the whole of Greece. It affected painting, sculpture, mythology, theology, and mysticism. The most striking phenomena came in the early phases of the movement, before the rise of 5th century Athenian culture.

As far as the psychosocial setup, it was in style very different from, say, a Victorian séance. Creating Dionysiac miracles was a wildly chaotic and bizarre enterprise. Sometimes it was mortally dangerous. In addition to Dionysian mania,[57] the people of Elis left accounts of controlled experiments in the materialization of wine. The ancient Greeks, superlative in magic, mysticism, and mythology, also created the basic logical tools necessary for rational, scientific thinking. The genius of the ancient Greeks was manifold.

In the beginning, the cult of Dionysos was improvisational. A combination of three items was needed to evoke the epiphany of the god: flute and dance, a state of ecstasy, and the maenads—the ecstatic women enthralled by the music and dance magic of Dionysos. This was a dance cult largely for women acutely disposed to cut loose from their confined, domesticated reality. The sound of the flute triggered the nocturnal dances that became increasingly frenzied and that gravitated upward toward the mountain tops.

The bacchantes of this nocturnal revel left their normal personalities behind. As the Greek word *ek-stasis* indicates, they were "outside" themselves, figuratively and literally. Their old selves were definitely submerged and displaced, and in a supernaturally exalted state, they acquired uncanny powers. Suddenly invested with superhuman strength, they tore trees up from the ground. They seized the fleet deer and the quick leopard, and ripped them apart with their bare hands. The rocks and the streams around them came to life, and milk and honey gushed from earth and stream. Everything confined was unlocked, the hidden became manifest, the impossible broke open into reality. These orgies of ecstasy were ultimately healing rites, despite the occasional collateral damage to life and property. At their peaks of mania, the god himself would manifest; here we might speak of collective apparitions, perhaps like those reported of the god-bearing Madonna in modern times.

To understand what the Dionysiac healing ecstasies were like, it is best to read the *Bacchantes* by Euripides and look at ancient Greek vase painting. Pentheus, a prince of the establishment, opposed the arrival of this cult that consisted of groups of women that appeared, by normal standards, to be quite mad. Conservative Greek society did not welcome the Dionysiac invasion of ecstatic, wildly dancing women in the throes of visionary experience.

Bacchantes tells the story of the conflict between male hegemonic rationality and collective feminist mania, a conflict joyfully triggered by the dancing god of intoxication and indestructible life. When Pentheus is caught spying on the maenads in ecstasy, they turn on him violently and tear him limb from limb. To add irony to tragedy, one of the entranced visionaries who dismembered Pentheus *was his mother*. In the back story, Pentheus had a long-standing issue with Dionysos, the god of the vine. Pentheus, in fact, was the archetype of prohibition and repression. He is therefore at mortal odds with Dionysos, who is the *Archetypal Image of Indestructible Life*, to use the title of C. Kerenyi's study.

Making the case for the reality of miracles of materialization, Walter F. Otto's *Dionysos: Myth and Cult* (1965) is of special interest. As I've been saying all along, the phenomena under scrutiny are found in all cultures and all histories. What we find is an ecstatic syndrome of puzzling effects. The god-possessed women—the Bacchae—draw milk and honey from natural streams of water. They poke the ground with a *thyrsos* or scratch it with their hands and wine or water gush forth. They are immune to fire and pain and poison and will not be bound by chains. The basket young girls are weaving suddenly blooms with ivy and grape vines.

Yet more spectacular were the marvels witnessed at the public festivals where the god-intoxicated women invoked apparitions of Dionysos and sacramental wine gushed from the ground while grape vines were observed to flower in a day. At festivals honoring Dionysos, the god appeared as an apparition, increasing the frenzy of the maenads and precipitating the miracles. At the god's birthplace, the Island of Teos, fragrant wine periodically gushed from the ground. At the festival in Elis, miraculous wine was confirmed by many witnesses. According to Pausanias, a contemporary historian, citizens and foreigners swore under oath that they witnessed these prodigies of nature.

Describing what must count as one of the first experiments in the parapsychology of religion, Walter Otto, in his book on Dionysos, writes: "…three empty basins were put into a room in the presence of citizens and any foreigners who happened to be present. The room was then locked and sealed, and anyone who wanted to could bring his own seal to add to the seal on the door. On the next day the seals remained unbroken, but those entering the room found that the three basins had been filled with wine. Pausanias assures us that the citizens and the foreigners vouched under oath for the reliability of the report." All this was part of the seasonal festivals. Otto continues:

"The most amazing miracle, however, was that of the so-called 'one-day vines' (*ephemeroi ampeloi*). These flowered and bore fruit in the course of a few hours during the festivals of the epiphany of the god."

These phenomena altogether were so compelling they penetrated the highest echelons of Greek philosophical and dramatic culture. "This was a miracle which commanded serious belief, a miracle which Sophocles and Euripides considered worthy of their praise. We do not intend to discuss it with the flippant remark that it was nothing but a hoax perpetrated by the priests." [58] It is hard to avoid the conclusion that the extraordinary spread of the Dionysiac cult was propelled by ecstatically induced miraculous perceptions. Instead of silently melting into the One, the maenadic disciples of Dionysos went out of their minds and danced on mountains at night and suckled wild animals, thus melding with the universal mother of living nature. In a form of nature mysticism, the maenads sought to transcend their ordinary, woefully male-restricted humanity.

Euripides saw the attempt to repress the ecstatic needs of the psyche as an offense to the god. Is there a message for us children of modern technology? Do we perhaps hold back from ecstasy for a reason? Do we fear unleashing forces we might not be able to control? Speaking of irony, Dionysos was the god who came to liberate humanity from repression, but it turns out that humanity has decided to do its best to repress Dionysos.

Intercontinental Flying Houses

Some long believed miracles have been proven false or strike us today as too absurd to entertain even for a moment. Still, the attachment to them may be so deep that we refuse to renounce them completely. Clinging to a particular miracle belief is itself a topic worthy of study. We might ask about the uses that belief in miracles serve; for some, clinging to the impossible is the only way to maintain sanity.

One miracle account that's not based on credible eyewitness testimony at least serves to illustrate the limber imagination of some miracle-prone cultures. Tertullian, the early Church father, took this bull by the horns when he wrote: "I believe *because* it is absurd." He was referring to the core Christian belief in the resurrection of Christ. We have to recognize a kind of creativity in an attitude that seems to say: "I believe, *no matter what*; it *shall be* true."

If there were such a thing as exercises for stretching the muscles of the imagination, for developing naïve credulity to genius level, the "miracle" of the House of Loreto would be a fine example. According to legend, in 330, relic collector Saint Helena found the house in Nazareth that the mother of Jesus had lived in, a "fact" confirmed by the Venerable Bede in 720. The Holy House, as it came to be known, stayed at peace until the Muslims invaded the Holy Land in 1291 when it disappeared from Nazareth on May 10, only to reappear at Tersatto, Italy, not far from the Yugoslavian border. The house was 31 by 13 feet and rose 28 feet. Made of reddish stone, the wooden roof was painted blue with golden stars. Inside were earthenware vessels, a wooden cross, and a cedar statue of Mary with the Divine Child. At first the people and the Pastor of the nearby Church of Saint George recoiled from the appearance of this little house from nowhere, fearing the work of the devil.

The Holy House remained for three years in Tersatto before it again vanished. Nicolas Fragipani built a small model of the original with the inscription: "The House of the Blessed Virgin came from Nazareth to Tersatto on May 10th in the year 1291 and left on the 10th of December, 1294." (I would not oppose creating a little cove in our Miracle Park where we could inscribe Fragipani's statement on a marble slab.)

On the very night of its departure, shepherds watching their flocks in Recanati, Italy, observed a house flying overhead that landed four miles away. There were so many bandits in Recanati, however, that the insecure house once again departed and finally found safe haven in Loreto where it continues to stand today, originally positioned at the junction of a road and a field.

Immediately after the Holy House landed in Loreto, Paul of the Woods, who was living on the slopes of Mount Urso, had a vision of the Virgin who filled him in on the house's origin and wayward travels. For centuries the devout rang bells and lit bonfires on the night of December 10 to commemorate the wanderings of the Virgin's Holy House along the eastern seacoast.

Within 16 years after this final translocation, Clement V issued a papal bull recognizing the Holy House, and German pilgrims began coming to make their vows at the new shrine. Napoleon's troops sacked the Holy House in 1797, stole the statue of the Virgin and Child, and installed it in the Louvre, but at the Pope's request returned it to the Loreto sanctuary. So many miracles were reported about the house that records were discontinued; it has become a major European shrine and yearly receives and entertains thousands of pilgrims. Many great saints made the pilgrimage to the House. In her autobiography, Saint Therese of Lisieux wrote: "How deep was my emotion when I found myself under the same roof as the Holy Family, contemplating the walls upon which Jesus cast his sacred glance."[59]

Since Clement V, forty-seven popes have in one way or another acknowledged the relic status of the House of Loreto. One week before convening the historic Vatican II, Pope John the XXIII went there to pray for success, and Pope John Paul II made a pilgrimage in 1979 just before his first visits to Ireland and America. Since the days after the house finally settled down in Loreto, Italy, numerous archeological and architectural studies have been made seeking to authenticate the House's globe-trotting trials and adventures.

Descartes, the father of modern philosophy, after having a dream that led to the discovery of analytical geometry, vowed to go on a pilgrimage of gratitude to Loreto. So we can add to the roster of pilgrims, saints, and popes, one of the great founders of the modern scientific revolution. The human imagination is fascinated by relics, and the history of the flying Holy House is surely one of the most fascinating.

The Parapsychology of Relics

From the Latin, *reliquiae*, relics are "remains." Relics play a significant part of religious life, and they are regularly linked to tales of miracles. The need for a vital connection with the spiritual power of our ancestors draws people to relics. Relics are a potent part of magic. The hair or nail parings of a person are relics that can be used for casting spells or for tuning into the mind of the person they came from. Australian *churinga* are ancestral objects that offer links to healing powers. For an extreme example, the ancient Celt coveted the head of a slain hero in hopes of obtaining the power stored in it. Meanwhile, contemporary psychic detectives like Noreen Renier reportedly gain impressions of crime scenes by touching an object that belongs to the missing or murdered victim.[60]

The remains of the cremated corpse of Gautama the Buddha were divided among eight followers. Several teeth, bones, and smaller fragments of the Awakened One have been preserved for thousands of years.[61] These and other Buddhist relics sit ensconced in thousands of stupas, or shrines, all over Asia, around which pilgrims, monks, and lay folk circumambulate in prayer and meditation. All religious architecture is a form of reliquary, as indeed the small constructions that house relics, called reliquaries, are often fine works of art.

The ancient Greeks were aficionados of the relic: Plutarch describes the ritual transfer of the remains of Theseus to Athens. Epidauros preserves the bones of Asklepios. Bones are powerful relics. In the Old Testament, we find this story of a dead man. "They cast the dead man into the grave of the prophet Elisha, and everyone hurried off. But when the man came in contact with the bones of Elisha, he came back to life and rose to his feet" (2 Kings 13: 20-21). This is a constant: miracles about saving, renewing, expanding life. The Roman Catholic tradition is rich in relic lore; veneration of relics, however, is left up to individuals. No one is obliged to use or believe in them; tolerated as devotional supports, they're handy for remembering, evoking, and channeling spiritual power.

The Acts of the Apostles tell how the sick were healed by crossing the shadow of Peter and by touching cloths handled by Paul. May all this be explained by the modern (though still obscurely understood) placebo response? When Saint Polycarp was burnt at the stake in 156, his disciples wrote how they took up his bones, "more precious than jewels and finer than refined gold." With these relics they celebrated the anniversary of his martyrdom. The Eastern Christians zealously dissected and parceled out the bodies of saints. In 787 the Second Council of Nicaea ordained that all churches must install relics under their altars. The need for every religious community to establish a vital channel with the sacred past was duly underwritten.

The bodies of the saints of the West were fair game for relic hunters, and indeed the remains of many Western saints are scattered in different churches and cities around Europe. During the peak miracle Middle Ages, people were avid for relics. Relics were stolen, fought over, fabricated; it was widely felt that a concrete sensory link to spiritual power had to be secured, and so much the better to get its status officially ratified.

As for the attraction to relics, there is a mounting scientific literature on the power of the placebo. Belief in the efficacy or authoritative status of a medicine or medical professional is known by itself to have therapeutic benefits. The world-old popularity of relics suggests an instinctive understanding of the psychology of the placebo response. The medically based placebo response is related to a well-known effect in parapsychological studies: belief and disbelief in the production of psychic phenomena, the former known to enhance psychic effects.

There is a phenomenon dubbed "psychometry," an unfortunate term introduced by an American physician, J. Rhodes Buchanan. The idea is that memories become linked with physical objects, so that a sensitive might read memories in a rock, an old watch, or a locket of hair. Such an object is sometimes called a token, and mediums will often ask for a token-object, a ring, bracelet, or old fountain pen that belonged to a deceased person, as a way of tuning into that person's psyche. The memories are somehow linked to the token object, and touching, kissing, or venerating the object may open one's awareness to hidden sources of information.[62]

Reports of recipients of organ transplants bear out this odd notion of memory. In some cases, recipients are said to acquire the memories, feelings, and tastes of their organ donors.[63] In this novel medical circumstance, the "relic" is transplanted into a strange body.

Relics are vivid reminders of the need to cherish the poetics of *things*, the soulful potentialities of objects with memories that people in throw-away cultures may ignore. Antique lovers retain this sense of the soul of things, while the capitalist spirit that thrives on what Heidegger called *Neugier* (constant desire for novelty) has little taste for it. The title of William Denton's classic on token objects and psychic impressions is called the *Soul of Things*. It's a good phrase that defines the parapsychology of relics, the attempt to recapture the soul of things.

The Most Famous Relic

Perhaps the most famous miraculous relic is the Shroud of Turin, said to be the shroud in which the body of Jesus was wrapped and which is thought to have an image of Jesus impressed on it. Some believe the image was produced at the instant that the crucified prophet was resurrected. The Shroud of Turin is periodically in the news and has been the subject of television specials. It burst on the scene at the turn of the 20th century when Seconda Pia photographed the famous cloth and discovered that the image on it appeared to be a photographic negative. The cloth reveals an image, front and back, of a crucified man with features that suggest a figure of Jesus. Carbon dating tests are supposed to have placed the cloth in the 13th century. This test is now viewed as flawed, having made use of a piece of the cloth that was exposed to handling and a fire in the 13th century.

At best, if the test were valid, it would show that the Turin cloth was not the shroud of the historical Jesus. Apart from the fact that the carbon dating tests have been questioned,[64] certain properties of the image on the cloth are very puzzling. First of all, it is clear that the figure on the cloth was crucified through the wrists, not the palms, as typically represented in art. Why would a 13th century forger paint an image showing crucifixion through the wrists? It would be an unlikely thing to do and would automatically arouse suspicion. Also, the image on the cloth is not a painting but seems to have been made by an instantaneous burst of heat. Stains on the cloth indicate two types of blood flow, venous and arterial, at a time when Harvey's discovery of the circulatory system was still in the future, and the two types of blood flow were unknown. No artist of the thirteenth century could have distinguished these two forms of blood flow nor been able to paint such a convincing image of them. Other features of the Shroud are inconsistent with it being a fraudulent artifact, but I see no point in going on with all the details. Quite apart from the date of the cloth, the information contained on the image is incompatible with the belief that it is a painted scam. The Shroud of Turin is a good example of a permanent paranormal object. Its ultimate meaning remains an open question.

Miraculous Events that Shaped History

One measure of the importance of some miracle claims is their historical impact. Events or behaviors that at the time were (and perhaps still are) perceived as miracles, and that resulted in historical change, deserve special mention. A few perceived miracles had a huge influence on history. One thing is clear enough, the origins and periods of renewal of Christianity often involved events that were extraordinary and very difficult to explain.

Historians admit there was something uncanny about the rapid and triumphant spread of a movement initiated by a few Jewish outsiders who rallied around a crucified and apparently failed Messiah. A small ragtag band of visionaries, their words and actions, eventually became the basis of a new world religion. The rise of Christianity was marked by a steady stream of events and influences that were completely off the charts of normality. As Robin Lane Fox says in *Pagans and Christians*: "'Epiphany' and visionary experience seem a constant part of Christian life, from the first vision of angels at the Tomb to the continuing appearances of the Virgin Mary in the modern Catholic world."[65] The idea of a religious movement seeded by such a visionary encounter was also notable in the religion of Dionysos, which was underway by the 8th century BCE; so there are parallel formations that even overlap in time.

We read in Mark 16:5-7: "As they entered the tomb, they saw a young man dressed in a white robe sitting on the right side, and they were alarmed. 'Don't be alarmed,' he said. 'You are looking for Jesus the Nazarene, who was crucified. He has risen! He is not here. See the place where they laid him. But go, tell his disciples and Peter 'He is going ahead of you into Galilee. There you will see him, just as he told you.'" The resurrection is the master miracle and cornerstone of the Christian creed. Various arguments have been advanced to defend the belief. It is said that nothing short of the resurrected Jesus could explain how the scattered and defeated followers rallied their spirits and in the face of apparent failure became the nucleus of a new world religion. Without news of the resurrection, it is said, the early followers would have dispersed; the crucifixion alone would have left them deflated and defeated. Jesus would more likely have been perceived as an abject failure, a suicidal fanatic out of touch with reality. But belief in the resurrection, based on the reported appearance of the resurrected Jesus, would explain the success of the Christian movement. Something causing transcendent enthusiasm had to have rallied the defeated, bewildered, and disillusioned disciples, and inspired them to become the historic apostles of a new world-movement.

The Conversion of Saint Paul

Another highlight in the miraculous beginnings of Christianity was Saint Paul, who was transformed by a visionary encounter with Jesus. Saul of Tarsus started out aggressively hostile to the new sect of Jesus followers. The story of Saul's conversion to Paul the foremost missionary, if not the founder of the movement that produced Christianity, is documented in the Acts of the Apostles and in one of

Paul's letters to the Corinthians. The transformation, or change of mind (*metanoia*), had many of the earmarks of a typical near-death experience.

In the second letter to the Corinthians (12:2-4), Paul wrote (alluding to himself): "I know a man in Christ, who fourteen years ago, was caught up—whether still in the body or out of the body, I do not know, God knows—right into the third heaven... into paradise and [who] heard things which must not and cannot be put into human language." In the Acts of the Apostles (9:3) we learn, referring to the same event, that "suddenly a light from heaven flashed around him" and, falling to the ground, he heard the voice of Jesus: "Saul, Saul, why are you persecuting me?" We have the ingredients of a near-death experience,[66] an encounter with the mystic light, and ecstatic out-of-body experience, which Paul interpreted as a visit to the "third heaven." The experience, recalled 14 years after the fact, made a profound impression and was the immediate cause of his conversion. Paul, more than Peter, was responsible for bringing the Christian gospel to the Western world. Converted to the new faith, he became its greatest early apostle. The psychical transformation of Paul of Tarsus was a key event in the spread of a new world religion.

In This, Conquer

The spread and gradual advance of Christianity in the ancient world took hundreds of years. The process, as the historian Lane Fox reminds us, was riddled with visionary, psychical, and miraculous experiences. The Gospels, apart from their revolutionary ethical content, were filled with stories of miraculous healings, exorcisms, and other supernormal events. One event of great significance, which hastened the death of the old deities, was the conversion of the Roman Emperor Constantine. This, in effect, would result in the official triumph of Christian archetypes over the Western mind.

In Britain, where Constantius Chlorus died in 306, Constantine, his son, was proclaimed Emperor by the army. Constantine was only one of several claimants to absolute power in the Empire, and remained so until 312. Everything changed when he invaded Rome and won the battle against Maxentius at the Milvian Bridge. Magic played a role in ancient warfare, and Maxentius was supposed to have relied on using omens, sacrificial magic, and the Sibylline prophecies to fend off challenges and keep his rival Constantine at bay. Constantine also needed protection and was on the look-out for divine allies. A record of a pagan speaking out before the Emperor states: "To be sure, Constantine, you have some secret contact with that divine mind which entrusts care of us to the lesser gods and deigns to show itself to you alone..."[67] Expectations were high and the battle was perceived in light of the higher, hidden players in the great game of empire.

Exactly what happened on the day of the battle remains obscure. Ancient historians tell us that before the battle, Constantine and his troops saw a light and a cross in the sky. Also, in a dream vision he was told to inscribe the "heavenly sign of God" on his warriors' shields. The "sign" consisted of a cross made of the Greek letters *chi* and *rho*, the first two letters of the name Christos. Under oath, Constantine described his vision to Eusebius, his friend and the early Church historian. Constantine swore that he and "all the troops" saw the "sign of the cross" and the words "By this, conquer" in the noonday sun; so he instructed his soldiers to paint the "symbol of the cross" on their shields before entering the fray.

Maxentius was quickly routed, and Constantine emerged as the chief power of the Roman empire. This led to a turning-point in world history. The Emperor declared the Edict of Milan in 313, which mandated toleration of all Christians, ending the persecutions and martyrdoms. After 300 years of missionary labors, the underground Christian movement was about to acquire structure, respectability, and power. The journey from miracle to bureaucracy had begun.

The historian Jacob Burckhardt considered the talk about miracles in the sky mere fantasy; in his view, Constantine was driven by a cold calculating will to power, and simply exploited the new rising Christian *zeitgeist*. However, after Constantine secured power and became "Augustus," he still launched a cathedral building project across the Empire, and evidence suggests a genuine attraction to the new religion in addition to his real power-hungry motives.

Constantine did not blossom into a model Christian and even murdered one of his sons for political reasons. The conversion of the empire was a slow process, a changing of the gods that scarcely took place overnight. It was an evolution of religion and politics, pagan and Christian, often shaped by visionary experiences and claims of miraculous encounter.

An Unclassifiable Miracle

Edward Gibbon published *The Fall and Decline of the Roman Empire* in 1776, a book religionists attacked for its hostile stance toward Christianity. However, while busy lambasting all the "pious frauds," Gibbon interrupts his narrative and writes: "Yet the historian who views this religious conflict with an impartial eye, may condescend to mention *one* preternatural event, which will edify the devout, and surprise the incredulous."[68]

Tipasa, a maritime colony of Mauritania in Northern Africa known for the zealous orthodoxy of its people, had fought off the Donatists and the Arians. Most of the Catholic inhabitants had fled by boat to the coast of Spain from the onslaught of a heretical bishop. Hunneric, who was in Carthage, sent a military dispatch to Tipasa, and the rebellious Catholics were arrested. Brought before the inhabitants of the province, their right hands were cut off and their tongues cut out. A grim premise for a miracle story.

The sequel was attested by the African bishop Victor Vitensis in a publication two years after the event; apparently, they whose tongues had been excised *continued to speak.* In Tipasa, about 70 individuals who had their tongues removed continued to produce articulate speech. Gibbon accepts the historical testimony for these strange events and uses the word "miracle" to describe them, quoting Victor: "If anyone should doubt of the truth, let him repair to Constantinople, and listen to the clear and perfect language of Restitutus, the subdeacon, one of these glorious sufferers, who is now lodged in the palace of the emperor Zeno, and is respected by the devout empress." According to this report, the phenomenon was ongoing, there were multiple witnesses, and the witnesses were credible.

Gibbon was astonished to find "a cool, a learned, and unexceptional witness, without interest, and without passion," the Platonic philosopher Aeneus of Gaza, who described his observations: "I saw them myself: I heard them speak: I diligently inquired by what means such an articulate voice could be formed without any organ of speech: I used my eyes to examine the reports of my ears: I opened their mouth, and saw that the whole tongue had been completely torn away by the roots; an operation which the physicians generally suppose to be mortal."[69]

Gibbon refers to further evidence for this astonishing report in an edict issued by Justinian, an account in Marcellinus's *Chronicle* of the times, and one of the dialogues of Gregory the Great. The enemies of Catholic orthodoxy, Gibbon notes, are prevented by an "incurable suspicion" from accepting the most "plausible evidence" for any Catholic miracle. Why? As Hume had observed, to admit such "miracles" would seem to authenticate Catholic orthodoxy and empower the dreaded Papism. Gibbon, who was anything but a Papist, saw this; still, he chose to include in his history an account of at least one report of something utterly strange and singular, with eyewitness testimony of what Gibbon himself called a miracle.

The Conquest of Mexico

Besides the murderous talents of Cortez, a miraculous image helped to convert the native Aztecs to the religion of their conquerors. The story began on December 9, 1531, a dozen years after Cortez invaded and imposed his will on the native population. Peasant Juan Diego, an early convert to the Christian faith, was on his way to hear Mass celebrated in the village of Tlatilolco. Passing by the base of a hill called Tepeyac, which was the location of a former Aztec Mother Goddess shrine, he heard a bird singing. He looked up at the summit;

a voice was calling him in his native Nahuatl. Diego saw a strange light, then an Indian-looking girl who said she was the Virgin Mary. She urged him to hasten to the Bishop's palace in Mexico City. She wanted a temple erected for her on the hill of Tepeyac.

After entreaties from Diego, Bishop Juan de Zumarraga politely asked for a sign. So Diego, during a second appearance of the mysterious young girl, explained the bishop's request. Proof of her divine identity was required. Then, on the frost-bitten hilltop, Diego noticed Castilian roses in full bloom. He was instructed to cut and wrap them in his cactus-maguey tilma, bring them to the bishop, and repeat the demand for a temple.

Diego found his way back to Mexico City and explained to the bishop his latest encounter with "the Lady from Heaven." Then he loosened his tilma and emptied the roses on the ground. Another surprise awaited all: the cactus cloth of Juan Diego now bore a life-size, brightly-colored image of the girl who appeared to him. The bishop was nonplused and everyone fell to their knees.

News of the miraculous image on the tilma spread quickly. *Within ten years, about nine million Aztecs converted to the new Christian creed.* The image was a propaganda coup for the missionaries. The Aztec population was now spiritually beaten by the Spanish conquistadors. Unlike the (periodically) bloodthirsty deities the Aztecs were used to, the new virgin goddess beckoned them more gently to holiness. She appeared to Diego's mortally sick uncle and reportedly healed him instantly.

All this sounds like a fairytale, but it's well-grounded in historical fact. As early as 1560, a document based on Nahuatl sources and written testimony of Bishop Zumarraga was produced to authenticate it. Again, in 1666, a formal investigation of the tradition concluded in favor of its authenticity. In 1924 a Peruvian document known as the Codex Saville was found that confirmed the Guadalupe image as dating from 1531.

Twentieth century scientists examined the image of the Indian girl's eyes and claimed they saw faces reflected in them, presumably

Diego and Zumarraga. The magnified texture of the Virgin's eyes work like Rorschach blots; believers see what they want in them. Still, some features of the image are puzzling. Artists who examine the tilma find no brushwork or other indications of how the image was produced. More telling, the colors of the image have not faded despite its great age. By contrast, parts of the cloth surrounding the face that were touched up show unmistakable signs of decay and darkening. Further, and most provocatively, the cactus cloth should have rotted away in 20 years; it has survived intact for centuries. Infrared photography proves there was no under-drawing; the cloth had not been sized, which, if true, could have at least partly delayed rotting.[70]

The image of this solitary feminine figure is everywhere in Mexico. She stands on her own, without cradling the infant Jesus. Like the old Aztec Goddess, though in a less blood-thirsty guise, she stands proudly in her own form, a sovereign force that has shaped the inner history of Mexico—myth or miracle—a spiritual power that captured the soul of the people.

Toward Superphyscial Transformation

Looking at the growing array of anomalies, a picture begins to emerge of a radically evolved human body, a body with extraordinary properties such as levitation, bilocation, inedia, creative materialization, and much more. Imagine what it would be like to be free from the constraints of gravity, if you could be in more than one place at the same time, if you could live without eating or drinking, if you could see into the hearts and minds of others, if you had an expanded time consciousness, and could, if necessary, scan directly the past and the future. Imagine also that you intuitively perceive and feel the oneness hidden beneath the bewildering and sometimes terrifying diversity of other human beings. Imagine, finally, a radically transformed perception of existence: a moment to moment, new consciousness of life. This seems to be the emerging picture: information that enlarges our view of the possibilities of human existence—a balm, I hope, to the limping imagination that feels beaten by reality and contracted by hard if not catastrophic times. On now to the first of a definitely off-beat cache of high aspiration oddities.

The Incorruptibles

There are strange accounts of the incorrupt bodies of saintly men and women. The phenomena–dead bodies that remain perversely reluctant to show signs of decay—are grotesque and bizarre.[71] Nevertheless, if miracles are a language, we will have to ask what *this* phenomenon is trying to say to us. Let's look at a gaggle of incorruption effects.

For one, a teasing fragrance persists around these crepuscular corpses for months or even years, as was the case with St. Teresa of Avila and Joseph of Copertino. Second, the bodies of certain heroically sanctified people remain flexible after death; not lapsing into "cadaveric rigor," as Thurston puts it. Third, they remain immune to decay, sometimes for hundreds of years, hence called incorruptible. This, of course, is after saponification, embalming, or desiccation are ruled out as explanations. A very odd feature is that after weeks, months, even years, these incorrupt bodies may suddenly spurt warm blood. Months after her death, the body of St. Catherine of Bologna was exhumed and bled from the nostrils before several witnesses. More rarely, warmth, even intense heat, may persist long after death. Then, finally, in the words of the great Jesuit scholar himself: "There are a few cases in which the dead saint is alleged to have raised his arm in benediction, or lifted his foot to be kissed, or turned his head towards the Blessed Sacrament, or covered the pudenda when the body was being reclothed."[72] I'm fond of the black humor of the foot being lifted for a kiss and of the laughable irony of a corpse covering its pudenda.

One of course wonders what it was about the lives of these heroic seekers of sanctity that could conceivably account for their after-death cadaveric antics. As far as I know, not a single attempt has been made by church or science to investigate any of the prodigies of bodily incorruption. A scientific study of incorrupt bodies might seem like desecration, but who knows what new knowledge awaits the intrepid investigator?

Like dreams, many miracles seem to dramatize or materialize an idea or a symbol. Copertino's levitations are physical metaphors of his inner flights of ecstasy. Likewise, the stigmata are physical metaphors of identification with the suffering Lord. In the case of bodily incorruption, the phenomenon seems a metaphor of the resurrection: physical demonstrations of a power that retards decay and entropy, preserves the form of life, and even intoxicates us with heavenly perfume. Some might see the smile of the universe in these mysterious gestures of rebellion against the brute fact of bodily death.

Hindu saints, like Christian, exhibit the phenomenon of bodily incorruption. Yogananda is a modern Hindu example; the witness was a Los Angeles Mortuary Director, Harry T. Rowe. After 20 days, according to Rowe, the body of the Hindu saint remained fresh and unaltered by any signs of decay, claiming that the case of Yogananda was "unique in our experience."[73] Miracles like bodily incorruption and levitation are transcendent images of life, as are the stories of miraculous healings.

Rainbow Body of Tibetan Buddhism

Amazing are the feats of the human body, watching, for instance, the world's greatest gymnast, Simone Biles, leap and somersault through space with a grace beyond anything I've ever seen. But there are much stranger phenomena, also pushing against the known limits of the possible, for example the rainbow body of Tibetan Buddhism. Involved here are effects that seem the opposite of what happens to saintly Christians. Instead of the dead body remaining fresh, fragrant, and flexible, insisting on the appearance of life, the dead Tibetan body begins to shrink and get smaller and smaller and then disappears without a trace.

The phenomenon has been decribed first hand in a fascinating book by Francis V. Tiso entitled *Rainbow Body and Resurrection*

(2016). Tiso learned Tibetan and tracked living witnesses of a recent case of the Lama Khenpo A Chö, who died in 1998. Tiso uses a translation of a brief biography of this Buddhist holy man who taught and practiced meditation almost incessantly with the one goal of immersing himself in the void of "primordial awareness."

Tiso was able to interview four witnesses of the death of Khenpo and of the contraction and disappearance of his corpse. As customary, the body was covered with a yellow sheet and placed in a box for one week, after which it was supposed to be cremated. Many monks and lay people where he died also witnessed some of the more spectacular phenomena.

Khenpo died with his rosary in hand as he recited his mantra. "Immediately after that all the appearance of bodily aging (he was 82) such as wrinkles, shriveling, etc., instantly disappeared. His face became youthful—smooth and pinkish." The fragrance normally detected about Khenpo suddenly increased. All the people nearby making prostrations noticed what Christians call the odor of sanctity. "Above his house," again from an eyewitness, "five colorful rainbows appeared for many days. Sometimes they pervaded the whole expanse of the sky, as was directly witnessed by all the monks and lay people of Lurap." Toward sundown of that first day a sunlike light appeared in the east, "and was seen by all of us." In addition to the rainbows, "after three or four days, they heard a very melodious song" but no source of the music was found.

Tiso asked all four witnesses about the shrinking and disappearance of the body. Their answer: "The body was shriveling. It was becoming smaller and smaller. On the spot, it disappeared." It was turning whiter and whiter. The complete disappearance was established by observation on the eighth day. By that time the body had completely dematerialized. All that remained were rainbows, mysterious music without words, a fragrant presence—and the yellow cloth that had covered his body. Not a hair or a nail clipping of the man remained. Such is the case of the Tibetan rainbow body at death.

How to account for the difference between the Catholic phenomenon of the incorruptible body and the Tibetan Buddhist phenomenon of the rainbow body? I would suggest the cause of the difference lies in the different philosophies. The one tradition celebrates a vision of a glorious spiritual body in heaven being our fate; the other tradition focuses on the symbol of the void and total detachment from all things finite and particular. Both approaches point perhaps to complementary visions of enlightenment.

One last observation about the politics of enlightenment: While Tiso was interviewing his witnesses, he discovered that Sonam Puntsog, who wrote the short biography of Khenpo quoted above, was jailed by authorities. The state apparently was uneasy with the idea that miracle-making human beings like this actually exist—I wonder why.

Medical Miracles

Bernadette of Soubirous was told she would find a healing spring—and scratching around by the caves of Massabielle her hands discovered a spring just below the surface of the ground. Since then Lourdes and its springs and grottoes have become famous and people from all over the world have been coming in quest of miracles or to serve the needs of the sick pilgrims.[74] Various emotional, spiritual and psychosomatic healings apparently take place at this sacred locale.

An international medical bureau tests the claims of those with unexplained recoveries; the criteria the doctors use are up-to-date and very stringent. There must be evidence that the subject was suffering from incurable disease, the cure must be instantaneous, and it must be permanent. No surprise that few claims withstand such strict criteria, and yet the fact is that so far the Lourdes Medical Bureau has certified about 70 cases said to pass this very stringent muster.

A striking feature of cases of miraculous healing reported at Lourdes involves persons who regained a function in spite of dysfunctional organs. In Gerad Baillie's case, the examining doctor wrote: "The child has chorioretinitus with double optic atrophy. He should not see." But apparently after Lourdes his vision was restored.

A similar optical enigma is reported of the case of Gemma di Giorgi, a girl from Ribera, Sicily, who was born without pupils in her eyes, and was therefore blind. But the girl's grandmother took her on a trip to San Giovanni Rotundo in 1947. At the end of mass, they attended with a crowd of people, Padre Pio was heard crying out, "Gemma! Come here!" She approached him, and he, smiling, told her she had to receive her first communion. While hearing her confession, the Padre stroked her eyes gently with his hand. After receiving the sacrament, Gemma and grandma bumped into the Padre again, who said to Gemma: "May the Madonna bless you!"—at which utterance Gemma cried out loudly that she could see! The cure was permanent, and so was the absence of her pupils. Many physicians have testified to this case for which there is no scientific explanation.[75]

The story of Pierre de Rudder is instructive, and is told in detail by Georges Bertrin.[76] De Rudder broke his left leg, which didn't heal and left him in agony for eight years. The Viscount du Bus gave him, his wife, and two kids a place to live on his estate and provided for all their needs. Moreover, the Viscount brought many of the best physicians to treat de Rudder, but none were able to provide any help, baffled by the un-healing gangrenous state of his dangling broken bones. After eight years of misery that evoked so much attention and sympathy, on April 7, 1875, De Rudder had finally gotten permission from his liberal (nonmiracle-believing) benefactors, to go to Lourdes on crutches with his wife—in hopes of a miracle.

After a difficult and painful trip, and dead tired, he sat down on a bench at Oostacker near a statue of the Blessed Virgin. He remembered his prayer. It was simple. He pleaded for relief from his invalid condition, so he could work for his family and make their lives easier. Almost immediately it happened; shocked and amazed, de Rudder stood up and found himself walking without a trace of pain. A two-inch-thick strip of fresh bone had instantly materialized and all the step by step stages of the normal healing process of tissues instantly achieved. The documentation for this story is abundant: that on the 6th of April many knew of and saw de Rudder in the state he had been for eight years, incapacitated by an unhealed, chronically painful, suppurating broken leg, but the next day, the 7th and after his prayer experience before a statue of the Virgin Mary, de Rudder had his leg back, renewed to perfection. All this is attested to by many witnesses and physicians with photographs and written reports. After his death, the autopsy revealed the newly materialized, whiter part of his leg bone.

The Gospels are full of accounts of healing, performed not just by Jesus but by the apostles; cases where the blind reportedly see, the dumb speak; the lame walk; lepers and paralytics are healed, and the dead are raised. In 2011 Craig Keener published a massive, scholarly, two volume study called *Miracles: The Credibility of the New Testament Accounts* in which he challenges "the prejudice of Western antisupernaturalist" interpretations of all miracle claims.[77] The unique value of these volumes are the numerous stories of miracle claims that are garnered from all over the world, and not only in Christian communities. The author is careful not to assess the exact truth value of the claims; he wants mainly to argue for the massive and persistent reality of claims similar to those made in the New Testament and for the possibility of asserting their 'supernatural' status.

Reports of medical miracles have continued until contemporary times. Jacalyn Duffin, physician and historian of medicine at Queens University, Ontario, drawing on the archives of the Vatican library, has reviewed four centuries of testimony that bear on the topic of "medical miracles."[78] The idea for this research came to her after she was invited to examine the medical records of a patient in remission from acute leukemia. Only later did she discover this patient's story was part of the canonization process of the first Canadian-born saint, Marie-Marguerite d'Youville. By "a medical miracle" Duffin means a healing that contemporary science cannot explain.

There is a good reason for focusing on medical miracles; they can more clearly be ratified or rejected in light of modern science. The phenomenon of miraculous healing is stable across history, according to Duffin, although there are changes of emphasis; for example, in modern times more doctors are brought into the process of certifying the miracle. I agree with Duffin who thinks that healing miracles speak to something universal in the human condition.

The process of certifying who is a saint keeps evolving and has kept pace with the ethos of the modern world. The thinking of the popes and the physicians has become more refined; nevertheless, *i processi* (examinations of testimony) continue to bear miraculous fruit. So it appears, according to Duffin, that we have a robust phenomenon worthy of study. Among the 1,400 cases she studied from the Vatican Archives, ranging from 1588 to 1999, a total of 48 countries from Australia to Uruguay were represented.

In saint-making, science and religion embrace temporarily, uniting in their submission to evidence—the *positios* (bound testimonies), *dubios* (doubts, questions), and *riti processi* (ritual processes). The physician does not pronounce a healing miraculous. Her only duty is to give the best scientific account of it; if she gives a credible explanation of the "miracle," it will be discarded or laid aside. If she or he cannot explain the healing, the door remains open for the Church to adjudicate its status as a miracle.

Duffin devotes a chapter to the supplicants. Who are the people who plead for and receive miracles? Of the four centuries of cases studied, the majority were common people of all classes and ages; one notes the inclusivity of these miracles. The miracle-happening is a product of many contingencies. "A potential saint can be invoked only by those familiar with her deeds and reputation." Miracle-making, in these accounts, is a byproduct of tangible locales and experienced intimacies.

Duffin describes a woman in agony, supplicating a being she believes, begs, and hopes will heal her; a powerful image of what religion is about at its wrenching core: the soul *in extremis* crying out for help, one's life on a wing and a prayer. The woman in this story had a huge, hard tumor in her left breast. "For twenty days and nights, Maria prayed to the uncanonized Paolo, witnessed by the woman who shared her bed." The pain continued, but by morning the tumor had vanished. In looking at the data in support of the cause of the saint,

Duffin implicitly lays the groundwork for theorizing the origin of religion. For surely such experiences are bound to generate strong "religious" or "spiritual" beliefs.

Most of the miracles in the author's database involve inexplicable, often very rapid cures of diseases ranging from cancer to tuberculosis. Miracles of this type apparently go back to the early gospels. The tradition continues on through Medieval times (when the cult of Mary inspired new waves of miraculous performance), and steadily into the twentieth century, in spite of the growing sophistication of medical science.

Duffin looks closely at one key player in the drama of miraculous certification: the doctor. "I quickly learned," she writes, "that the Vatican does not and never did recognize healing miracles in people who eschew orthodox medicine to rely solely on faith." The alleged miracle needs to be tested by reason, observation, and the whole web of customarily justified beliefs; only in light of these do we have standards for calling something "transcendent" or "paranormal" or "miraculous."

Duffin documents the growing importance of the physician in the miracle-certifying process. The number of doctors involved has gradually increased over the centuries. The maximum number of physicians involved in assessing a single miracle was 19 in 1926, as part of testimony for the "cause" of Joaquina de Vedruna, who was beatified in 1940. In some of Duffin's cases, doctors themselves were recipients of a miracle. She documents in detail the growing use of technology in the diagnosis and therapeutics of miracle cases, emphasizing the scientific credentials of the process. "Miraculously cured patients were treated with the best modalities available, be it drugs or surgery." In a curious ex-voto painting. we observe a man obtaining radiation therapy as he invokes the Virgin, looking over him from a cloud formation in a corner of the room. Examples are cited of drugs and surgery being rejected by supplicants who were nevertheless miraculously healed.

The doctors are not all believing Catholics; many are Jewish or nonbelievers. Disagreement among doctors over an alleged case in effect "falsifies" the miracle claim. Sometimes there are rivalries between doctors, which adds to the democratic élan of the process. Some doctors resist the very idea of miracles but in the end are key players in the saint-certifying process. Personal differences must be laid aside in forming medical opinions, for ". . . doctors serve as essential witnesses from science," observes Duffin, "the polar opposite of religion." So the attempt to certify miracles is willy-nilly an attempt to unite science and religion.

What about the criteria for a miracle? The healing must be "complete, durable, and instantaneous." Extraordinary speed of recovery was frequently encountered, and is often what makes the physician throw up his hands, and say, "I can't explain this; it's beyond the reach of science."

Miraculous healings are often highly dramatic. In one case, doctors had given up on an infant whose death they said would occur in moments, and indeed the child seemed to have expired. The mother in desperation swifts the child away to the tomb of the nearest saint. "Then she fell on her knees, sobbing and praying fervently to the spirit of the saint inside, asking him to intercede with God to spare the child's life." An hour or so later, the child revived, restored to health; community and witnesses gave joyful thanks.

Sometimes the whole family prays for intercession near the entombed body of a saint. Spiritual transcendence is rooted in the concrete, the sensuous, the particular: it is *this* lock of saint's hair that is coveted for its spiritual power. The journey to the tomb of the saint was often arduous, thus intensifying the felt appeal for help. The tomb of the saint, the pilgrimage there, the relics, novenas, images, vigils, sacred lamps, and anointing with oil—all served to focus and heighten the drama of miracle-making. Duffin details the role of dreams and visions, and ends by discussing the importance of thanksgiving in the miracle drama. In conclusion, Duffin's study asserts the stability of miraculous healings through the last four centuries. Clearly, we're not looking at some fly-by-night anomaly.

Prayer, Speed, and the Therapeutic Word

Underlying some miraculously sudden healings is a truly astonishing placebo effect. Bruno Klopfer of the University of California, Los Angeles, wrote a paper entitled "Psychological Variables in Human Cancer," which tells the story of a "Mr. Wright" who was dying from cancer of the lymph nodes, which were the size of oranges, but he was convinced that a new drug called Krebiozen would cure him. When he received the drug, the tumors melted away quite quickly, and he was cured. The dying man walked out of the hospital in good health and lived well for months until he heard news that the drug was not effective. He lost his trust, his faith in Krebiozen, and the cancer came back with a vengeance.

His doctor understood what was happening and gave him the drug again, insisting the correct dosage was the real McCoy. Mr. Wright believed, and again the cancer rapidly disappeared, and again he lived well for months, flying planes for fun, until finally he heard the latest report on the worthlessness of Krebiozen. Despite his fine health, Mr. Wright took this to heart, no longer believed, and the cancer came back. This time he died. Remarkable is the astonishing speed of his belief-induced healings and his belief-induced relapses. High speed healing—contrary to customary nature—suggests a miracle in church doctrine. Here we have the story of a man who was "miraculously" healed by believing in Krebiozen, a horse serum with no medicinal value. It looks as if what really counts is the act of believing, not necessarily what you believe in.

Prayer is another non-conventional healing method; physician Larry Dossey has documented many stories of miracle by prayer.[79] The common form of prayer is to call for supernormal assistance for oneself or others. Intercessory prayer is found in all cultures; appeal to a higher agency to intercede on behalf of some need, request, or desire. In recent times, experiments have attempted to prove that intercessory prayer works. If modern research proves that it does, we are in a better position to understand why religious belief stays strong, despite the onslaught of secular science and reductionistic ideologies.

People offer petitionary prayer—and beyond the obvious auto-suggestive and coincidental benefits—it sometimes seems their prayers are answered. When it happens, it provides positive feedback for one's belief system. If nothing happens, it too has value; it can be construed as a test of faith.

The research on prayer seems to show that prayer works. But are the results due to the paranormal talents of humans, or to the deities our ancestors believed in? Or some combination of both? One obstacle to receiving belief-induced health benefits is exerting too much egocentric effort, which can sometimes be self-destructive. Effortless intention is a better way of courting the benefits. The psychological strain of believing that I must somehow evoke a miracle may impede the effects. Belief in God, on the other hand, or belief in my patron saint, guardian angel, or rabbit's foot releases me from any inhibiting sense of responsibility. In handing over our miracle needs to the Higher Ones, we reduce egocentric involvement and effort; we get out of the way, we let it happen. Part of the irony of miracle making is that we have to completely forget ourselves before we can do what we might be capable of.

Effective prayer, and other miraculous gambits, depend on the co-creativity between ourselves and something outside ourselves. The something outside us both needs us *and* completes us. God needs us to fully manifest what God is all about (which of course we can never fully know). It raises the possibility of a new kind of experiment, a new kind of attitude toward "God," one touched on in a book by Nikos Kazantzakis, *The Saviors of God.* The secret is that God needs us as much as we need God. The divine adventure is co-creative, a dance between our personal minds and the great mind, the infinitely unknown part of ourselves that we cannot escape or ever fully fathom.

The parapsychology of God is perhaps a topic whose time has come.[80] There were moments in history when the various conceptions of divinity were born and began to take shape. They did so in and through the psychic energy of visions, dreams, apparitions, and other ecstatic flights of imagination. Certain uniformities of experience appear across the cultural divide. While there is the resurrection body in the Christian tradition, there is an Indian tradition of the Maha-Siddhis, the "perfection of the body and the non-obstruction of its functions by the elemental powers."[81] In both traditions, forms of radical concentration of mental powers are key to producing phenomena we designate at miracles.

In the *Yoga Sutras* of Patanjali, on *siddhis* or supernormal attainments, one word keeps popping up: *samyama*. Samyama means intense concentration. The siddhis or attainments are achieved through *samyama*. By performing *samyama* on one's karma, one gains knowledge of the time of death; on friendship, one becomes the ultimate charmer; on an elephant, you acquire supernormal strength; on the gullet, there's mastery of thirst and hunger; on cotton balls floating in the wind, the high of levitation. And so on and so forth. *Samyama* is concentration so steady, so complete, that you forget yourself and get lost in the image, thought, or activity concentrated on. The focus is extremely persistent and all-absorbing.

"Concentration" is one of the marks of the "clever man" in aboriginal Australian life. "He began to concentrate his thoughts in the manner of a sorcerer, to harm him," is written in a narrative of an aboriginal invoking the Dreamtime. This psychological variable turns up in curious places. The ability to concentrate attention for prolonged periods on goals, images, and outcomes is of interest to a theory of miracles.

If even a fraction of the reports discussed in this chapter are grounded in matters of fact, we should feel the need to rethink assumptions about the general character of reality and causation. The relationship to our own minds becomes more problematic; it's hard to be sure about the limits of our minds and the possible connections with other minds. To explore the world of miracles we need to crash out of metaphysical boxes. It's the worst kind of box to be stuck in, because you may not know you're in it.

Three: Beyond Physicalism

Science without conscience is mere ruination of the soul.

Rabelais

Miracles are critical to the story of religion, shamanism, and mysticism, but their reality today is doubted by most educated people. This is due largely to the rise of modern science with its bias toward material properties and measurability as essential criteria of *all* truth claims. Science has undercut the concept of miracles by explaining many things naturally that seemed at first supernatural but of course were not. Early peoples imagined thunder was a god shouting at them; meteorology put that belief out of court. And so it went.

But the amazing progress of science so far does not explain everything in human experience. Nor does that progress justify the repression of "miracles" and anything hinting of the paranormal. In part, the early deconstruction was valid. Pierre Bayle's *Various Thoughts on the Occasion of a Comet*, published in 1682, was a case in point.[82] Bayle's Enlightenment ethos, which demystifies puzzling features of nature like comets, influenced Voltaire and Thomas Jefferson, who in turn sought rightly to expurgate superstition from politics. The hope was to end political domination undergirded by outmoded beliefs; Bayle was laying the groundwork for the separation of church and state.

In a 17th-century Europe teeming with stories of miracles and witches, science might seem to offer a new, more predictable and fear-free explanation of the world. It would no longer be possible to mystify and terrify an ignorant public, it was optimistically supposed; science would destroy the belief-systems that kept the masses ignorant and defenseless against the cunning of tyrants and bullies. Unfortunately, science and technology in the 21st century have not saved the world from dictators, war, or false consciousness.

And still there are reasons some might resist certain paranormal ideas. Telepathy, for example, could be seen as implying the loss of one's inner privacy; if we accept telepathy, we would have to admit that other people might be able to "read" our minds, snoop on our innermost secrets, fantasies, and obsessions. Psychokinesis too might be resisted because it suggests that black magic and sorcery could be effective; it would remind us of how vulnerable we might be to subtle and perhaps unsavory influences. At the risk of losing our privacy, we would be exposed to new types of malevolent intentions. For these reasons, people of paranoid disposition might demur at the idea of telepathy and psychokinesis.

Others might recoil from the afterlife hypothesis because it would force them to revise their basic idea of how to live. It might awaken old fears of hell that were drummed into them when they were children by punitive parents or hell-and-brimstone preachers. Some people might resent having to admit they were wrong about a worldview they had become emotionally comfortable with; sheer laziness and arrogance might also conspire to keep others entrenched in their narrow views.

David Hume on Miracles

Philosopher David Hume's essay on miracles exhibits a distinctively political form of resistance to the paranormal. His infamous essay on miracles calls attention to a contemporary outbreak of truly strange phenomena, a series of events enmeshed in a bitter controversy between Jansenists and Jesuits.[83] On May 3, 1727, Deacon François de Paris, a Jansenist known for his sanctity, died, and on that day the first healing miracle ascribed to his spirit was reported. The deacon's gravesite became the scene of numerous bizarre "miraculous" phenomena, lasting for years and spreading to the environs of Paris. Supernormal healings were widely reported, but they were overshadowed by a different class of often grotesque physical phenomena produced by the so-called "Convulsionaries" of Medard. The extreme behaviors of the deacon's votaries were understood to demonstrate the power of spirit over the body. Besides the reported healings, other displays consisted of eating ordure and sucking on the suppurating wounds of sick people; the convulsed ecstatics that performed these bizarre feats not only enjoyed their repast but were demonstrably invigorated.[84] Innumerable witnesses observed and wrote about these truly surreal happenings.[85]

Historian Ronald Knox was by no means a friendly commentator, describing the deacon as a man with an "instinct for starvation and squalor and complete self-obliteration." But nevertheless, he describes at length the reality of the strange and "miraculous" phenomena. Knox quotes from one witness: "You saw in the cemetery of St. Medard, men falling like epileptics, others swallowing pebbles, glass, and even live coals, women walking feet in the air . . . . You heard nothing but groaning, singing, shrieking, whistling, declaiming, prophesying, caterwauling."[86]

One thing all, even Hume, agreed upon: the Convulsionaries of St. Medard behaved in astonishing ways; their physical performances defied normal explanation. The Jesuit enemies of Jansenism were forced to yield to the facts as attested by so many witnesses. Hume's reaction to what were being called "miracles" is what concerns us here.

It was an age of revolution and *philosophes*, and the new materialism had political consequences. According to this view, the enemy of science was organized religion and superstition, things we must be ready to resist for the sake of truth, progress, and enlightenment. But, as the English scholar John Donne said, all "coherence" was gone with the rise of this new cosmology. A new coherence was rising, and it seemed to require getting rid of the mysterious, the mystical, the supernatural. Miracles became a code word for anathema, the enemies of science and political progress. The only miracle was what "man" could accomplish by means of unfettered reason.

Miracle claims so disturbed Hume that he hoped to devise an argument in his 1748 essay to "be an everlasting check to all kinds of superstitious delusion, and consequently, will be useful as long as the world endures." Talk about overrating your accomplishments! He begins with the reasonable Humean claim that experience is our best guide to the truth of matters of fact. Agreed. Facts may be rare, ambiguous, elusive; or obvious, repetitive, and weighty. "A wise man, therefore, proportions his belief to the evidence." For witnesses to a phenomenon, "the evidence, resulting from the testimony, admits of a diminution, greater or less, in proportion as the fact is more or less unusual."

Notice that Hume did not say, as some modern anti-psychists do, that "extraordinary claims require extraordinary evidence," which is nonsense. The claim that Joseph of Copertino levitated is extraordinary; the evidence for his levitations was not extraordinary at all, but consisted of people who saw with their own eyes the man rise into the air in the same way they would have attested to the fact that a bird had entered a church and flown about.[87]

Hume hoped to make an argument that would once and for all silence anyone with a "miracle" claim. "A miracle is a violation of the laws of nature; and as a firm and unalterable experience has established these laws, the proof against a miracle, from the very nature of the fact, is as entire as any argument from experience can possibly be imagined." The first dubious assumption was that all the laws of nature were known; moreover, it is un-Humean and unempirical to assume that any "law" is based on "unalterable experience."

With a little sleight of hand, Hume rules out, *a priori*, any event that cannot be comprehended under the *known* laws of a given epoch. But this is a formula for squelching new and radically surprising matters of fact that turn up in human experience, and blotting them out of any possible scientific purview. If Hume were right, we would have to discard every new phenomenon that was inconsistent with familiar patterns of past experience—a perfect formula for impeding scientific progress. We learn what is matter of fact solely from experience and can't *absolutely* be sure even that the sun will rise tomorrow, however well established and customary the experience of daily sunrise. Inductive knowledge is not absolute knowledge. In fact, sometimes knowledge grows in proportion to the knower's willingness to deviate from existing norms, and pursue matters that are puzzling and uncertain.

Zeal to combat superstition and "enthusiasm" deformed Hume's reasoning, blinding him to matters of fact that clashed with his beliefs and political preferences. But Hume places before his readers the evidence needed to refute his claim about the phenomena of St. Medard: "There surely never was a greater number of miracles ascribed to one person, than those, which were lately said to have been wrought in France upon the tomb of Abbé Paris, the famous Jansensist, with whose sanctity the people were so deluded. Curing the sick, giving hearing to the deaf and sight to the blind, were talked of as miracles of the holy sepulcher. More extraordinary, many of the claims were immediately proved upon the spot, before judges of unquestioned integrity, attested by witnesses of credit and distinction, in a learned age, and on the most eminent theatre that is now in the world. Nor is this all: A relation of them was published and dispersed everywhere; nor were the *Jesuits*, a learned body, supported by the civil magistrate, and determined enemies to those opinions, in whose favor the miracles were said to have been wrought, *ever able distinctly to refute them*" (italics added).

Hume adds a lengthy footnote providing further details in support of the extraordinary claims, including some useful bibliographical references: "Many of the miracles of Abbé Paris were proved immediately by witnesses of the officiality or bishop's court at Paris, under the eye of cardinal Noailles, whose character for integrity and capacity was never contested even by his enemies." The new archbishop did not favor the Jansenists, but Hume reports that "22 rectors or *cures* of Paris, with infinite earnestness, press him to examine those miracles, which they assert to be known to the whole world, and indisputably certain."

Hume then criticizes (we are still in his footnote) the Molinist (Jesuit) party for unfairly repudiating the healing of Mademoiselle le Franc, but who "soon found themselves overwhelmed by a cloud of new witnesses, one hundred and twenty in number, most of them persons of credit and substance in Paris, who gave oath for the miracle." Again, to underscore this: one hundred and twenty witnesses, most of whom were creditable persons, testified under oath that something inexplicable had occurred.

We are told of a "Mons. Heraut, the *Lieutenant de Police*, whose vigilance, penetration, activity, and extensive intelligence have been much talked of. This magistrate, who by the nature of his office is almost absolute, was invested with full powers, on purpose to suppress or discredit these miracles; and he frequently seized immediately, and examined the witnesses and subjects of them: *But never could reach anything satisfactory against them*" (again, italics added).

And neither does David Hume say anything satisfactory against the reports he has before him of the extraordinary happenings at St. Medard. What then does he conclude from all this? Returning to the main body of his text we read: "And what have we to oppose to such a cloud of witnesses, but the absolute impossibility or miraculous nature of the events, which they relate? And this surely, in the eyes of all reasonable people, will alone be regarded as a sufficient refutation." And so, all the sensory observations of numerous, highly credible witnesses—placed in the balance with Hume's *belief of what is impossible*—are reduced to nothing! And surely Hume picked a loaded metaphor when he spoke of a "cloud of witnesses" for the view he was attacking. A breeze can disperse a cloud. A more accurate and telling metaphor would have been "mountain of witnesses."

How to explain this slippage into self-contradiction, this reversion to pig-headed dogmatism? Hume was bewitched by a word, *miracle*, which he defines as something "absolutely impossible." Because witnesses and participants of the Medard phenomena used the word *miracle*, which for Hume meant "violation of the laws of nature" and "absolutely impossible," reports of them became in his eyes automatically incredible, no matter the quantity or the quality of the testimony.

Hume reveals his deepest anxiety when he writes, " . . . we may establish it as a maxim, that no human testimony can have such force as to prove a miracle, and make it a just foundation for any such religion."[88] Here it is plain what Hume's phobic reaction is all about; he is afraid of making a miracle the "foundation for any such religion." Hume fears the possible exploitation of "miracles" by some religion, e.g., the Roman Catholic. If he had dispensed with the politically charged terminology of "miracle," and if he were less fanatical about his opposition to religion, it might have been easier for him to regard the strange phenomena more objectively.

Rather than make an argument that forever silenced all miracle claims, Hume showed how a person in the grips of a dominant idea, however great a thinker and congenial a human being, may suffer from intellectual blind spots and blatant self-contradictions. Hume had the information before him about all the extraordinary phenomena associated with the so-called Convulsionaries (in fact, not all the phenomena were accompanied by convulsions). Intellectual honesty forced him to present a fair account of events, which, however, he concluded were based on some kind of delusion. He described the facts and the testimony in support of them accurately, but refused to credit them as actually true. This fairly common effect I call *Hume's syndrome*, a kind of involuntary negative hallucination with regard to seeing or acknowledging facts that appear to disrupt one's cherished worldview.

Hume's syndrome is not to be treated lightly. Bayle, Voltaire, Paine, Jefferson,[89] and other Enlightenment stars all associated prodigies, wonders, miracles, and the supernatural with political and intellectual backwardness and oppressiveness. This attitude still undergirds much of the irrational resistance to the paranormal. Moreover, there are some factual reasons for calling attention to this fear, but rational caution differs from hysterical rejection. Occultists, spiritualists, wiccans, Forteans, and psychical researchers are traditionally attacked, ostracized, and sometimes demonized by the scientific elite and, for different reasons, by organized religion. Hume's syndrome shows up in many shapes and guises.

A Pope Pioneer of Parapsychology

An 18th century writer who introduced a more rational attitude to the study of "miraculous" phenomena is Prosper Lambertini, who was not only a papist but a pope! Before becoming Pope Benedict XIV, he served 20 years (1702-1722) as *Promotor Fidei*, otherwise known as the Devil's Advocate. The role of Devil's Advocate was to cross-examine witnesses and critically examine evidence for miracle claims and heroic virtue. Legalistic jousting was part of the beatification and canonization processes. Admired for his tolerance, humor, and practical scientific rationalism, Lambertini's job was to determine if an alleged miracle (paranormal occurrence) withstood critical scrutiny. Based on his experience as Devil's Advocate, he published a four-volume study *On the Beatification and Canonization of the Servants of God* (1734-8).[90]

What we find in Lambertini, unlike Hume, is a willingness to confront the entire range of human experience. Lambertini drew on common sense, history, knowledge of human nature, and the widest possible compass of recent scientific knowledge to determine if a claimed phenomenon could be explained in terms of known natural science. Comets and falling stars were treated as intelligible in terms of the new astronomy. There is discussion of what today we call altered states of consciousness in the production of supernormal cognition. Since witnesses often claim that saintly persons emanate or are surrounded by preternatural light, he provides a detailed discussion of unusual natural luminosities. To determine what counts as normal for a period of time that one goes without food or drink, he assigned a Dr. Beccari the task of collecting all the known information on the subject, and ended by doubting that preternatural fasting was proof of divine influence.

Likewise, he reviewed all the available data describing the natural circumstances in which a dead body may remain incorrupt, and concludes there are cases that defy scientific explanation. But Lambertini denies they are proof of holiness. Without using contemporary terminology, he clearly understood that some illnesses are psychogenic or psychosomatic, and therefore healing them may not be miraculous in the sense of entailing divine intervention.

He fully grasped the role of imagination and its possible pathological or therapeutic effects on the body. Without using current lingo, he understood the concept of placebo. He arrived at almost impossible criteria for "miraculous" healing, demanding that healings be sudden, complete, and lasting before they qualify as miraculous. Lambertini must be counted an early pioneer in the scientific study of supernormal phenomena.

History is full of surprises and contradictions. Hume, a philosopher of genius and radical exponent of experience, is blinded by his assumptions and uncritically cashiers whole domains of human experience. On the other hand, Lambertini, a titular embodiment of bugbear "Papism" is fair, rational, and objective in treating the same outlaw phenomena. So much for stereotypes.

Are Poltergeist Events Miracles?

The word *poltergeist* in German means *noisy spirit.* We need to underscore the variety of shapes and forms that poltergeists assume. There are cases of water poltergeists, water apparently gushing from nowhere, fires starting without apparent cause, and projectiles thrown about by invisible forces. Poltergeists used to be thought the work of spirits, or the antics of devils; now it seems that adolescents under emotional stress may be the unconscious agents of these well recorded outbreaks of high strangeness.

Similar dynamics are probably at work in both the phenomena of statues and paintings that weep and bleed and the more anarchic outbursts of the multi-faceted poltergeist. Of notable strangeness in poltergeist phenomena are manifestations of matter penetrating matter, whether it be nails locked in a cabinet reappearing in all parts of a house or stones from outside entering through walls into the living rooms of a house. At least some of these phenomena are most likely the unconscious products of humans under stress; the phenomena seem to externalize impulses that have no other outlet. But to my mind it's not clear where the mischievous energy is coming from. When the poltergeist acts up only in the presence of a particular person, we assume the source of the psychic mischief lies in that person. It has, however, been suggested that the poltergeist person only furnishes the emotional energy that a spirit siphons from the presumed poltergeist agent. There are, in fact, poltergeist cases where there are no young, emotionally charged persons around to be the unconscious agent of the poltergeist.

In the 1960s, a famous poltergeist showed up at a law office in Rosenheim, Bavaria. Weirdness proliferated: ceiling lamps swung back and forth, ink was ejected from cartridges, the phone system registered numerous phone calls to ascertain the time, and the office took on the look of a funhouse rigged with tricks. Architects, physicists, electrical engineers converged on the scene. All were duly baffled. They concluded there were unknown forces registering physical effects everywhere in the vicinity of the office.

The disturbances occurred only in the presence of a young worker, Annemarie Y. When she arrived at the workplace all hell broke loose. When she was removed to a new workplace, everything stopped at the old but began again at the new. The "miracles" seemed to be emanating from Annemarie, not from God or the devil.[91]

In another age or culture, the same young woman and her poltergeist might have been canonized as a saint or burnt as a witch. It seems there are many unpredictable ways a thwarted mind can end up expressing itself. As I suggested previously, there are similarities between poltergeists and bleeding and weeping statues and paintings. The similarity lies in the role that stress plays in producing these uncanny phenomena. As for the mechanism whereby blood or tears are materialized de novo, or teleported from somewhere, or whereby stones in a poltergeist pass through solid matter, we are almost clueless. These miracles, religious or secular, leave us speechless and dumbfounded.

Mesmerism and Psychical Research

Before the 18th century, miracles were generally welcomed as testimony supporting religion, but since then they have become suspect and are now associated with bigotry and oppression. One way to resist the corrupt Church was to attempt, as Hume did, to invalidate all of the miracle claims. So the Enlightenment savants cultivated contempt for any and all claims of miracles, marvels, prodigies. An example of this newfound modernist scorn of miracles was Thomas Jefferson's taking a few nights off from his duties as president of the United States to expurgate all references to miracles from his copy of the New Testament. Jefferson thought Jesus was the greatest social moralist but tried to revise and modernize his image so that he resembled a miracle-indifferent 18th century *philosopher*. Like David Hume, Thomas Jefferson had a big pair of blinders on and refused to see the riot of anomalous phenomena that were taking place around him, in his own time and in France, a country where he managed to fall in love with a married lady.

The 18th century declared the triumph of reason and the end of miracles even as it witnessed the rise of Mesmerism and many new miracles of the human mind. Anton Mesmer (1734-1815) launched a new phase of research into human mental life, and a new phase in the history of various marvels. Mesmerism led to what is called the "discovery of the unconscious," as Canadian psychiatrist Henri Ellenberger, psychotherapist Adam Crabtree, and others have shown.[92] Mesmer sparked a zeitgeist that would spawn psychoanalysis, hypnosis, psychical research, analytical depth psychology, and transpersonal psychology—a line of research that opens the door to the reportage of "miraculous" phenomena. Frederic Myers, William James, Charles Richet, William Crookes, Carl Du Prel, Leo Morselli,

Alfred Russell Wallace, and many others were drawn to psychical research. This train of radical empiricist research ran parallel (though increasingly in the shadows) to the reductive empiricism that grew from the Humean outlook and its obsession with control and predictable uniformity.

A Dictionary of Miracles

Not surprisingly, different cultures elicit different types of miracles. Australian aboriginal "clever men" in their open spaces were good at clairvoyance. The telekinetic movement of the hosts and other claimed Eucharistic miracles are peculiar to Catholic culture. Whereas, *tummo*, or the heat generating yoga unique to Tibet, is at least in part elicited by a cold forbidding climate. The phenomenon of metal-bending and claims of alleged voices of the dead picked up on magnetic tape are rather recent European and American effects associated with new technologies. According to psychologist Kenneth Batcheldor, our expectations contribute to what we are likely to produce in the way of psychic effects. If true, we need to think about how to cultivate and control states of mind conducive to psychic effectiveness. We need to learn *how* to expect, *how* to be open to extraordinary phenomena with confidence. As far as I can see, human miraculous potential, if rightly conceived and anticipated, may in the end turn out to be virtually limitless.

To gain a sense of the range and variety of phenomena, a quick scan of Ebenezer C. Brewer's *A Dictionary of Miracles* provides a collage of examples. Welcome to our Miracle Park. So, from A to Z, drawing on scripture, biography, history, and hagiography, Brewer provides reference after reference, illustrating the copious miraculous mind and imagination. Following Brewer, here are some descriptive phrases, in alphabetical order—a sprinkling of unusual and impossible human behaviors—*alleged*, we must say.[93]

Consider this Multiple Miracle Billboard: Aaron's rod becomes a serpent; angel visitations; angels carry souls to paradise; angels entertained unawares; angels sent for consolation; apparitions of the dead; Christ appears to St. Catherine of Genoa and gives her a ring of betrothal; apparitions of the Virgin Mary; apparitions to give directions about dead bodies; aureole or glory; the face of Jesus shining like sun during transfiguration; St. Philip of Neri's face lighting up after receiving the sacrament; barren women becoming mothers; bibliomancy (using the Bible like the I Ching for divination purposes); bleeding paintings and weeping statues; blindness miraculously cured; burning bush; chains falling off prisoners; Christ in the form of a child visits St. Antony of Padua; churlishness supernaturally punished; compacts with the devil; candles consumed but not diminished; conversions in large numbers; cripples healed; crosses in the sky (the emperor Constantine); the dead speaking, hearing, moving; the dead raised to life again; delivered from prison; demoniacs possessed; devils assuming diverse forms; doves; dragons, subjected and subdued; dreams, warning and prophetic; Elisha called Baldy summons bears to wreak revenge; fig tree withered by miffed Jesus; fire innocuous (immunity to fire); flowers and fruits from paradise; food multiplied; garments that heal; gates opening of their own accord; gift of tongues; gravitation, increased or diminished; guides enigmatic and unexpected; lifted up (levitation); lions that behave gently; miracles of doubtful morality (St. Hilary murders his daughter by prayer to keep her from the snares of the world); prophetic warnings; relics (ebullition of the blood of St. Januarius); trance and ecstasy; visions and revelations; water supplied (Elijah and Black Elk make rain); and so forth.

Actually, this (highly abbreviated) list is a mixed bag. The story of Elisha being teased for his baldness and turning wild bears on his tormentors seems like a nice example of miracle black humor. Some seem clearly incredible, like Magdalena de Pazzi jumping up from being dead and spinning around like a Sufi trance dancer. There is almost always an edifying message, a piece of propaganda, or an ad for the absolute. In some instances, however, there is credible eyewitness testimony. Let's have a look at one interesting example, a recurrent phenomenon steeped in symbolic significance.

Marian Miracles

Visions of the Virgin Mary were first recorded in the 11th century in Walsington, England. Since then they have been a recurrent phenomenon, starting to accelerate in France and Italy around the time of the French Revolution and continuing up until the present, occurring everywhere on Earth. Two spectacular visionary events of the 20th century are definite reality-benders: one in Portugal at the time of the Russian revolution in 1917; the other in Zeitun, a suburb near Cairo, Egypt, in the late 1960s, when tensions between the Muslim Brotherhood and the Christian Coptic minority were high.

Let's begin with the 1917 appearances of the Virgin to three children in Portugal. "At Fatima, Portugal, on October 13, 1917, seventy thousand people witnessed one of the greatest miracles of all time."[94] In this story, a Lady from heaven told three children to come back to the same spot, a certain cove, every month. The Lady said that on the last day of her appearance she would perform a miracle for all to see. In the ensuing months, the children were questioned, detained, and persecuted, and the case reported in the international press; Portuguese anti-clericals came out in force to monitor the scene and bring down the young imposters.

On October 13, during a World Series hubbub in America, the children turned up at the Cova da Iria at noon with a huge entourage of humanity, along with a hostile press ready to pounce. A heavy rainstorm was sweeping across the countryside when suddenly it stopped, the clouds were rent and the sun appeared. Someone shouted in panic and looked up: The Sun appeared to be spinning on its axis, emitting flashing, rainbow-colored lights. To the horror of the crowd, the sun seemed to dislodge itself from the sky, assume a disc-like form, and plunge downward in zigzag fashion toward earth. The terrified crowds fell to their knees, in postures of supplication, believing the end was at hand. Astonished faces were captured on film, with looks resembling those of New Yorkers photographed on September 11, 2001, gaping at the flaming Twin Towers.

The falling “sun” disc stopped short of hitting the ground and zigzagged back up the sky into the position of the Sun, where it spun back into place. The countryside dried up from the heat of the disc, and healings of people watching from a distance were reported. A flabbergasted press was compelled to report what they saw, and to this day nobody can explain what happened. Some have noticed that the falling disc at Fatima behaved like reported UFOs sometimes do, especially the characteristic falling zigzag motion.

Fatima seems to have been a hybrid miracle, straddling the phenomenologies of BVMs (Blessed Virgin Marys) and UAPs (Unidentified Aerial Phenomena). Although none but three children saw the Lady, about 70,000 people witnessed the spinning disc phenomenon, the “miracle” on that October 13 of 1917, predicted six months in advance. The Lady promised something extraordinary would happen that day; she seems to have kept her word. The power of this story is twofold: The correct prediction of a “miracle” six months in advance, which shows the phenomenon as part of a long-range plan. The second point of power are the 70,000 witnesses that confirmed the prediction and experienced the miracle. True, this was not a carefully controlled scientific experiment. It was something obviously beyond the grasp of science as presently evolved.

An Egyptian Lady of Light

One of the most remarkable Marian sightings occurred in Zeitun, a suburb outside Cairo, Egypt, occurring on and off from 1968 to 1971. It was long lasting—certainly for a Marian vision. The Zeitun phenomena had outstanding features. The first is the overwhelming degree of evidence in support of their objectivity. Unlike the majority of Marian visions, which are typically visible to one or a few or a small group of young people, the Egyptian “Lady of Light,” like Fatima, appeared to thousands if not millions. The appearances were prolonged, at first several times a week and for up to six hours at a stretch. Over the three years that the visions continued, their number and duration diminished. The appearances were photographed, sometimes looking like merely suggestive blobs of light and sometimes as fully formed figures, birds, but mainly in the shape of a woman that moved, bowed, and waved at the people. In prolonged collective ecstasies, Muslims mingled in peace with the Christian minority. The Muslims (who venerate Mary) had suspended all restrictions on public religious observance. It was a shared celebration of the divine feminine, and made for peaceful co-existence between Muslim and Christian, at least temporarily. Other inexplicable phenomena included reports of documented healings.[95] To confuse matters, a minority who were on the scene saw *nothing at all,* according to some experiencers I interviewed. The question therefore arises: what sort of entity can be photographed, seen by most people, but also, and at the same time, remain invisible to others?

So overwhelming was the reality of these appearances that the highest authorities in the Coptic Orthodox Church testified on their behalf, as *The New York Times* reported on May 5, 1968, which begins "Coptic Bishop among those who tell of apparition." A year later, April 2, 1969, the *Egyptian Gazette* reported on a ceremony with international attendance at the site of the appearances, the Church of St. Mary at Zeitun: "Although a year has elapsed since the apparition was first reported, yet it is still appearing. The most recent report of its appearance was on Friday, April 4, when it was seen for thirty minutes between the central dome of the church and the cross situated above the church fence. The apparition was seen nodding to a large number of people who stood outside the church."

Remarkably, this prodigy drew little scientific attention from Europe or North America. One Canadian researcher with a penchant for crude reductionism did cite the Zeitun appearances and attempted to explain the strange photic effects as the result of tectonic strain. There were light effects, but they were not random splotches as you would expect if they were the result of tectonic strain; the light in fact took the shape of a moving female figure in a garb that people associated with the figure of Mary. Photographs, plus innumerable eyewitness accounts, prove it. The critical fact about the shape the light had assumed was conveniently ignored. This is the standard procedure of deniers of supernormal phenomena: the repulsive data become invisible; a sheet is drawn over them—problem solved.

The tectonic theory cannot explain another Zeitun effect. The majority of the people who viewed this phenomenon were Muslims. Muslims venerate Mary. During that time, as now, there was considerable tension between the minority of Coptic Christians and the Muslim majority. The tension erupted into violence under the influence of extremists, and there were laws restricting the freedom of Christians to perform religious functions in public. So overwhelmingly real was the Mary-vision phenomenon that it caused the suspension of interfaith hostilities. Customary constraints upon the Coptics were dropped, and millions of Muslims and Christians went into collective trances of spiritual ecstasy, forgetting their differences, in the presence of the appearances. None of this is likely to have happened if all they saw were meaningless blobs of light; people saw (and photographed) a feminine light-form that moved about, interacted with the crowd, and prompted claims of miraculous healings.

Virgin appearances seem like reactions to existential threats to believers. The Fatima appearances occurred in a context of clerical and Marxist antagonism. The phenomena are like a group near-death experience. Instead of the individual nearly dying and seeing transformative visions, the culture is threatened with death and the people see transformative visions.

A Marian prophecy produced in Garabandal, Spain, in the 1960s, predicted a global visionary experience, a single moment in time when the entire consciousness of humanity is going to be flooded by a shocking transformative light. Perhaps the millions of visionaries of the Lady of Light at Zeitun for three years was a first attempt at such a scenario. The idea of some coming moment of global illumination may play itself out in ways we cannot anticipate or imagine, for as the good book tells us, we know not the day nor the hour nor the methodology.

Now to a vision of the Madonna with some useful advice.

Diet from a Lady of Peace

In 1981, before Yugoslavia was plunged into bloody war, six youngsters from Medjugore began having visions of a Lady who announced that she was the Blessed Virgin Mary. There are several firsts here. One is that the children grew up and continued having visions and auditions of the virgin, and have spoken around the world of their experiences. They have visions and auditions, anywhere, anytime. An enormous cult evolved from the Medjugorje experience, and a thriving pilgrimage business. Before all the atrocities erupted in Yugoslavia, the kids were getting a persistent message of peace from the *soi-disant* Virgin. On August 6, 1981, the word *mir*, or "peace," appeared in the sky as if an invisible hand were writing it. Numerous witnesses observed this. Medjugorje escaped the ravages of the Bosnian conflict.

There were many odd stories surround these events. One concerns seeing strange lights on the barren countryside—light being the earmark of all sorts of queer psychic happenings. Another was also strange; a Catholic priest I met on a plane said he was incensed at the whole idea of Marian epiphanies, which he linked to jingoistic trash and Catholic fundamentalism. Still, he bought a ticket for the pilgrimage, choosing to form his opinion from his own experience. As it turned out, he was forced to deal with a funny little miracle, trivial, but a stubborn fact he couldn't deny: a set of rosary beads he purchased in Medjugorje changed color during the flight home. The beads were unquestionably blue when he bought them, but by the time he got home they were yellow. Others have reported their rosary beads changing color after a pilgrimage to Medjugore.

Another novelty worthy of attention: the young visionaries of Medjugore were subjected to careful physiological studies during their experiences.[96] Professor Henri Joyeaux and Dr. Luigi Frigiero and his Italian colleagues investigated five of the visionaries. He tested them as a group while they were having visions and discovered that they were looking at the same point in space. They raised their heads simultaneously when the Virgin presumably appeared. They clearly behaved as if they were looking at some external "object."

They kneeled simultaneously; during the visions, which lasted from 3 to 45 minutes, all eye-movement ceased. Two of the subjects stopped blinking. None of them blinked in response to tactile stimulation of the eye. During ecstasy a screen was placed before the visionaries' eyes, and yet they continued to focus on the same point. Beholding the apparitions, cutaneous burns and lesions were inflicted on them, without response. Normal hearing was suspended, the subjects showing no physiological response to a 90-decibel input—which is equivalent to a loud explosion. During the apparition, their brains produced constant alpha rhythm—despite their eyes being wide open. A 1000-watt bulb lit before their eyes caused neither blinking nor change in alpha wave output. The pupil contracted, however, despite there being no sign that the brain was reacting to the light stimulus.

The investigators found no indications of abnormality in the visionaries. They appeared to be "partially disconnected from the outside world" and interacted with a being they alone could see and hear. The experience did not impair their perception of the external world, as one might expect if their condition was pathological. This is similar to deathbed visions of another world, which are negatively associated with drugs or other impairments of consciousness and do not disrupt normal perception of the external world.[97]

Professor Joyeaux and world renowned mariologist, Father Rene Laurentin, wrote of the Medjugorje visionary experience: "Just as the ordinary world is more real than the world of dreams, so too the Virgin is more real for them than is the ordinary world; she is not *unreal* but, rather, *surreal*. She does not belong to our space-time dimension; but can insert herself into this dimension, even if she belongs to another type of duration, the eternity of God."

The Transportation of Mrs. Guppy

Traffic is a growing problem all over the planet, so consider a story about a rare form of human transportation. If it ever became a reliable form of transportation, it would be the end of traffic jams. The form of transportation described here is teleportation; it fuses the apport (matter through matter) with levitation (matter unshackled from gravity). The speed of this futuristic means of travel is truly impressive. Instances of such transportation are admittedly rare, less common than levitations and rarer than instantaneous healings.

Time, place, and cultural environment are crucial to the occurrence of rare phenomena; the conditions have to be just right and must persist for some time. Extraordinary things might occur in spiritualist circles, for example, as they did in London in the late 19th century.

The miraculous transportation of Mrs. Guppy (Agnes Nicol) is a well corroborated case that took place in 1871. Mrs. Guppy was a talented medium that Alfred Russell Wallace took an interest in, and through his wife came to know and respect her unusual mediumistic talents. This was the Wallace who with Charles Darwin conceived the theory of natural selection and is known in history as the co-founder of the modern theory of evolution. Wallace was undoubtedly a great scientist, but unlike Darwin, he thought there was a spiritual dimension to evolution; hence his interest in mediums like Mrs. Guppy, who was a friend of the family. She was known to levitate and perform other astonishing feats that wildly contradict the reductive creed of materialism.

Her performance qualifies as a miracle that should indeed make you smile. So, on June 3, of that year, Mrs. Guppy, a memorably large woman, was transported from her home in Highbury, North London, three miles away to a house on Conduit Street where *10 witnesses,* two mediums and eight sitters, experienced her rather surprising arrival through the roof (Mrs. Guppy's matter through brick house matter)—the doors and windows of the house were closed. Remember, there are numerous reports of poltergeists in which rocks appear and disappear inside houses; it is a frequently reported feature of poltergeist experiences, solid matter passing through solid matter. If a stone, why not the magnificent Mrs. Guppy?

So, how did this curious event come about? Something trivial, or at best, amusing. One of the sitters in the house on Conduit Street asked the control during a séance to send someone from across town into their midst. (It was assumed in this group, apparently based on their experience, that such things were possible.) The séance at that point was being conducted in the dark. Another member of the circle suggested as a joke that Mrs. Guppy (known to this group) be fetched. A third person said, "Good gracious, I hope not, she is one of the biggest women in London!" Meanwhile the control replied to the request saying "I will."

Within three minutes someone cried out, "Good God, there is something on my head!" and there was a loud thump on the table and several screams. "A match was struck, and there was Mrs. Guppy on the table with the circle of sitters closely packed together . . ." In her slippers, she sat there motionless in a trance but then awoke, adjusted herself, and everyone else just carried on with the séance. "During this time, her boots, hat and clothes arrived from her home, also a lot of flowers." To imagine this happening is amusing but taxing even to my limber belief system. I struggle to see in my mind's eye Mrs. Guppy flying over London, followed by her clothing and personal effects.

Guppy's own séances were notable for the variety of apports they were said to generate. At her séances she produced huge quantities of flowers and fruits, showers of butterflies, of snow, of cactus plants, of live animals, eels and cats and lobsters, and then some. On one occasion, a friend of Alfred Russell Wallace asked for a sunflower and one dropped on the table out of nowhere that was six feet tall with clumps of earth attached to the roots.

Needless to say, all this boggles even the most elastic minds. But for three reasons this story strikes me as notable for its singularity. First, the fact that a great scientist (Wallace) vouched without reservations for Guppy. Second, there were many witnesses that confirmed the reality of Guppy's off-beat mode of transportation. And third, Frank Podmore, the arch critic of Spiritualism, was unable to account for Guppy's reported manner of transportation. There was no motive for fraud, he underscored—her husband was well off. In addition, there was no way to explain the quantities of the objects said to have been apported. If the narratives are true, and Mrs. Guppy was able to produce the various objects, in large quantities, and *on demand*, they certainly add to our picture of some wildly impressive latent human powers. I don't know what else to say about Mrs. Guppy.[98]

Sathya Sai Baba
Claims of materialization—of food, gems, sacred ash, and a good deal more—are made for the Indian spiritual master Sai Baba whose miraculous powers have repeatedly been observed, discussed, and sometimes repudiated as sleight-of-hand. The case is convoluted. It is known to careful students that authentic prodigies may co-habit with sleazy imposture. The best illustration of this mixed bag effect is the peasant miracle-maker from Naples, Eusapia Palladino. This woman produced baffling paranormal effects, as did the famous medium, D.D. Home.[99] Unlike Home, Eusapia was often caught in childish attempts to fob off fake results when inspiration failed, or when the insensitivity of investigators turned her off. Her performance depended in good part on the group dynamic, and when it was faulty, or when hostile and unsympathetic elements intruded, the phenomena failed and she sometimes resorted to crude deception.

Now this mixed bag effect shades into another point, found in the miracle lore of the Middle Ages and noted in recent studies by physician Larry Dossey who has shed light on the dark side of prayer; miracles, or any psi marvel, are not the sole preserve of the morally correct. There is good evidence that Sai Baba performed miracles; Psychologist Erlendur Haraldsson's well-documented study[100] presents ample eyewitness testimony that Sai Baba materialized physical objects *on demand*—rare fruits and unusual natural objects —performances beyond the pale of stage magic. But Sai Baba is also reported to have been observed cheating, although the photographic evidence for this is inconclusive.

Baba performed actions that were clearly of benefit in India for education and medicine. He also used his avatar status to prey on young men for sexual favors, according to self-declared victims. Whatever the truth behind these claims of moral defection, they imply nothing as such about his alleged miracle talents. It would be a mistake to assume that a talent for miracle-making is only possible if you're a morally impeccable person. It would be naïve to make that assumption, although it is true that much of the most powerful evidence for the paranormal is associated with people noted for heroic degrees of selflessness like Joan of Arc, Milarepa, and Arigo.

There are reports of Sai Baba materializing or multiplying food, as Jesus is said to have done. The curious part of these reputed culinary miracles is that the servings were produced hot: it is hard to imagine a magic act that required one to keep hot food up one's sleeve. Author and researcher Howard Murphet and his wife spent an extended period of time with Sai Baba and his community. Everyone that Murphet spoke with had stories of miracles to share with him. "My notebooks began to swell with fantastic stories…there were tales involving almost every kind of miracle found in the historic and spiritual records…the curing of many kinds of diseases, some deep-seated and chronic, some considered incurable by medical opinion." [101] Sathya Sai Baba was either a supremely gifted trickster or a fellow of awesome miraculous prowess.

Bhabutti or sacred ash is widely reported to materialize from his photographs around the world; I have spoken face to face with *several* apparently sane and credible people who claim they witnessed photos of Baba emit the sacred ash with their own eyes. How could Sai Baba use sleight-of-hand when he was not present at the site of the observed phenomenon?

Padre Pio and Future Man

During the Second World War the Americans had an airbase in Bari, about seventy-five miles from San Giovanni Rotondo, a village in

Southern Italy that housed a Capuchin friary. According to US intelligence, the Germans had a munitions facility in the hills nearby; an officer was assigned the job of bombing it. As the planes neared San Giovanni, the officer saw in the sky before him the figure of a monk waving him back. Dumbfounded by this spectacle, the officer ordered the planes to turn back. When the war ended, he went to the friary and met the monk who had appeared in the sky. His name was Padre Pio, who died in 1968. On a trip to San Giovanni Rotondo in 1979, I was unable to learn the officer's name or any details confirming this fantastic story. According to Father Joseph Pius Martin, an American friar in San Giovanni, the pilot lived in Florida.

Many incredible claims about Padre Pio (now St. Pio) are well-documented, but many are based on hearsay, part of the folklore that grew around the monk. In Padre Pio's world, ideas of fantasy and creatures of mythology came to life: Madonnas, guardian angels, shapeshifting demons, bilocation, magical cures, time-travel, and a good deal more. His story challenges rational commonsense and scientific assumptions of what is possible. Around the Padre, the incredible became certain, the impossible hit you in the face.

And yet, he was a human being. I assume therefore that his "miraculous" powers may well be somehow latent in all human beings. From early childhood Francesco Forgione lived in a world of visionary hyper-realities. At five he cried so much, especially at night, that his father once lost his temper and hurled him to the ground. Recalling these early years, Padre Pio said: "My mother would turn off the light, and a lot of monsters would come up close to me, and I would cry."[102] I was afraid of the dark when I was a child but my imagination was not as powerful as Padre Pio's. Padre Pio said of these early experiences: "It was the devil who was tormenting me."

Terrifying visions continued throughout his life, along with his more agreeable higher visions. Raptures, ecstasies, often lasting hours, in which his senses were suspended, occurred frequently. We know of these from his letters and from observations of his spiritual directors such as Father Agostino who eavesdropped on the Padre's conversations with invisible beings.[103] These included Jesus, Mary, Francis of Assisi, and his guardian angel. Agostino's *Diary* conveys the intense reality of Padre Pio's visionary encounters.[104]

Padre Pio's internal environment was infested with dark hostile forces. The higher visions were preceded by shapeshifting diabolic apparitions: huge black cats, naked women who danced lasciviously before him, an invisible entity that spat in his face and tortured him with deafening noises, and an executioner who whipped him. According to one of his confreres: "Padre Pio was very alert to unexpected movements and sounds. He said that the devil appeared to him in all shapes. He had fear even of a mouse, because the devil would start out as a mouse and turn into a claw and go for his eyes."[105]

These encounters produced physical effects. In Pietrelcina, claw marks and splattered ink spots were visible on the wall made by the alleged demons. Once, the iron bars of the monk's cell were found twisted out of shape after a night of grappling with invisible forces. Although no one beside the Padre ever saw the demons, the din they made was often heard by eavesdropping monks. More striking yet, Padre Pio was often found unconscious, sometimes on the floor beside his bed, covered with bruises from the assaults. It's a little difficult to believe he was doing all that to himself for theatrical purposes.

A well-witnessed event occurred in July 1964. A possessed woman was dragged to San Giovanni, and when she saw Pio, she cried out in an unnaturally deep voice: "Pio, we will see you tonight." That night the friars thought the house was struck by an earthquake. The Superior rushed to Pio's room and found him on the floor, bleeding from the head. Oddly, there was a pillow under his head. Pio explained that the Madonna put it there. In the morning, the possessed woman (undergoing exorcism from another priest) shrieked: "Last night I was up to see the old man. I hate him so much because he's a fountain of faith. I would have done more, except the Lady in white stopped me." According to Schug, this account was based on eyewitnesses not disposed to sensationalism. Pio's face was so disfigured he was unable to appear in public for five days. I have seen photographs of his face covered with welts and bruises. On another occasion he was found with broken bones in his arms and legs.

The attacks lasted throughout his long life. In 1918 he wrote: "I cannot describe to you how those wretched creatures were beating me! Several times I thought I was near death. Saturday it seemed as if they really wanted to finish me...." (*Epistolario*, III) Sometimes his afflicters came to him under the disguise of his spiritual director, Father Agostino, or as an apparition of a saint or guardian angel. Padre Pio had a technique for exposing these sinister masquerades; he would ask them to make the sign of the cross. If they did not, he inferred they were from the dark side.

Readers are bound to be skeptical about these reports of demonic assault. One might turn to Wilhelm Reich for an explanation. Reich believed such experiences were the result of repressed orgone energy turning against oneself. Or we might invoke the pathology of poltergeist phenomena to explain Padre Pio's demons. I am not certain how smoothly these explanations fit the story of this extraordinary man and his phenomena.

But there is one point I want to make about "demons" and the project of higher evolution. It does appear, as a matter of psychological fact, that in the quest for the highest states one often encounters agents of opposition who have to be dealt with. The story of the Buddha struggling to meditate on the Immovable Spot under the Bo Tree is a classic Eastern illustration. In Pio's case, the combat occurred at two levels. Throughout life he was molested by invisible "diabolic" forces; he was also persecuted by jealous, envious, and malicious human beings, often individuals within the church hierarchy. Ennemond Boniface has gone so far as to argue that certain individuals in the church were responsible for the priest's death.[106]

The Padre, however, did have some allies. His alleged "guardian angel" was no slouch, and was the saint's translator of French and Greek languages Pio was unacquainted with. Paranormal comprehension of Greek is more impressive than French, the latter being in many ways similar to Latin and Italian. In 1912, Agostino, by way of experiment, wrote letters to Pio in French and Greek. When Pio received them, he was at Pietrelcina for medical reasons, under care of a parish priest, don Salvatore Pannullo, who wrote on August 25, 1919: "I, the undersigned, testify under oath, that when Padre Pio received this letter (a letter in Greek and in the Greek alphabet), he explained its contents to me literally." When I asked him how he could read and explain it, as he did not know even the Greek alphabet, he replied: "My Guardian Angel explained it all to me." Agostino also confirmed Pio's ability also to comprehend the letters written in French.

Apparently, guardian angels are well-rounded in their education; they apparently also know something about automobile mechanics. In 1959, a woman was driving with her husband from Rome to San Severo. (The couple preferred to remain anonymous.) En route their car broke down; for two hours cars sped by without stopping. Toward nightfall, the woman grew anxious and began to pray to Padre Pio. Within 10 minutes a black car pulled up, and an elegant young man dressed in blue stepped out. He lifted the hood of their car and said: "Look, you lost all the water from the radiator, and it's burnt out. Take your can and fill it up with water. Near here, there is a farmhouse, which has a well; take the water from there."

The husband took the can from the car trunk and did as the young man said. The man then took a black box from his car, produced a roll of adhesive tape, and sealed the radiator. He had beautiful hands with agile tapered fingers. The dog, who normally barked at strangers, sat in the car's back seat, strangely calm. The husband returned with the water and filled the radiator.

"You can return home safely; anyhow, you are quite near," said the mysterious helper, who then got in his car and drove off. The couple watched the car pull away and looked for the license plate. There was none! Instead they saw a white strip marked with hieroglyphics. The car moved away slowly on Via Aurelia; suddenly it vanished.

Arriving home in a "dreamy state," they reflected on further oddities: The young man somehow knew there was an empty can in the trunk; also, that they lived "quite near." Later they tried to relocate the well and farmhouse but despite their efforts could not. There was no farmhouse in the area where their car broke down.[107]

Padre Pio also had access to other people's internal worlds. Like Saint John Vianney, the famous Curè of Ars, Padre Pio displayed supernormal powers of mindreading in the confessional. Hearing confessions was paramount in Pio's long ministry. Hour after hour, day after day for more than 50 years, he sat in a wooden booth and listened to people pour out their most intimate sins and secrets.

John Schug, who wrote one of the more critical books in English on Pio, tells of a confessor who intended to murder his wife. "Murderer!" Padre Pio roared in the church. The man skulked away and returned the next day, penitent and purged of his intention. Schug provides a detailed first-person account of Federico Abresch's confessional encounter with Pio. According to Abresch, a Lutheran convert, Pio recalled actions and thoughts he had long forgotten. "He enumerated with precision and clarity all of my faults, even mentioning the number of times I had missed Mass." Pio reminded Abresch of something he had forgotten years ago when he got married. In fact, it was only through Pio's remarks that Abresch was able to reconstruct his own past. Pio apparently had a more exact knowledge of Abresch's unconscious mental history than Abresch.

Abresch, by the way, regarded this as proof that something more than merely human "thought-transference" was involved. The fact that Pio could "read" the unconscious of another person seemed evidence of God's action, something totally beyond human capacity. But Abresch is mistaken. Evidence from mediumship and experimental parapsychology shows that telepathic leakage from another person' s unconscious does in fact occur. Once again I believe we are dealing with a general, albeit unrecognized, potential of the human mind, powerfully manifest in exceptional individuals such as Saint Pio, but phenomena that are still part of the natural (albeit mentally and spiritually expanded) world of human beings.

Padre Pio's access to internal environments enabled him not just to read but to change or convert minds. The Gospels portray Jesus as a man who took immediate psychic possession of his disciples. Pio too apparently had this ability. Consider an example from Schug. Unemployed Laurino Costa sent Padre Pio a telegram asking for prayer to help him find a job. The Padre telegrammed back: "Come to San Giovanni Rotondo at once." The young man arrived penniless and was standing with a crowd of men in the sacristy. Padre Pio, who had never met Laurino, shouted at him: "Laurino, come here. I see you have arrived." Bewildered, the youth approached. "Laurino, you will feed my sick." (A cook was needed in the new hospital.) "But Padre," Laurino protested, "I've never cooked an egg in my life." The Padre insisted: "Go and feed my sick. I'll always be near you." Laurino went to the hospital and rang the doorbell. The Mother Superior answered: "You must be the experienced cook we've been waiting for." Within three hours, he was at work. Laurino admitted to Schug: "To this day [14 years later] I still don't know what happened. All day long I found myself calmly working and telling others what to do, as though I was carrying out a routine I had been used to."

Mastery of Time and Space

Reports abound of Pio's double appearing everywhere, from the American Midwest to China and Africa. The idea of bilocation blatantly contradicts the belief that a human being is a physical object occupying one region of space. The idea that Jack could be at 42nd Street and Fifth Avenue in New York City and simultaneously at Main and Third in Sheboygan, Wisconsin, is obviously absurd. Nevertheless, the annals of saints, yogis, and psychics contain bilocation stories, sometimes well attested. Padre Pio bilocated by means of his voice, his presence, and his aroma; he appeared in people's dreams and sometimes he appeared fully materialized.

Mary Pyle, one-time secretary to Maria Montessori, spent the last 45 years of her life in San Giovanni Rotondo. In her diary she wrote: "One day I went into the sacristy and said to Padre Pio: 'Father, I believe my mother is in Florence today.' His immediate answer, given with certainty was: 'No, she is in Umbria.' Surprised I said, 'No Father, I do not believe she was supposed to go to Umbria.' But he insisted, looking far into space. 'She's been in Umbria.' A few days later I received a letter from my mother who told me: 'Thank Padre Pio for the visit he paid me while I was sick in bed in Perugia [which is in Umbria]. I did not see him with my eyes, nor did I hear him with my ears, but I felt his presence near my bed.'"[108]

Padre Pio seems to have known in advance he would be able to bilocate at a particular place. The Vicar General of Uruguay, Monsignor Damiani, a frequent visitor at San Giovanni, once told him he wanted to die in San Giovanni, assisted by Pio. The Padre said the Vicar would die in Uruguay but promised assistance anyway when the day of his passing came. In 1941, the Vicar died in Uruguay. Cardinal Barbieri was in the house where Damiani resided the night he died. Someone knocked on his half-open door. When he noticed a Capuchin friar pass, the Cardinal got up and went to Damiani's room. The Vicar had just died of a heart attack, but the friar had left a note on his dresser: "Padre Pio was here."[109]

Many bilocation stories revolve around healings. A typical example: on June 12, 1952, Lucia Bellodi, stricken with pernicious diabetes, was on her death bed when she sat up and began to wave her hands. She cried out that Padre Pio had appeared to her and told her she was cured and that she should come to his monastery. By June 16 she regained her speech and stopped having to consume 25 quarts of water a day. When she visited the Padre, he smiled and said: "I've been waiting for you."

A tantalizing case is that of Cardinal Mindszenty. According to a reliable Vatican source, he once received a "visit" from Pio while imprisoned in Communist Hungary. The monk, of course, was in San Giovanni, but his double turned up with water, wine, and altar breads, served Mass and vanished. When Schug wrote to confirm this from Mindszenty, he received back a one-sentence letter: "I cannot say anything about that." If the story were false, it's not clear why the Cardinal didn't say so, unless he meant to perpetuate a pious myth.

This form of bilocation, if it actually occurred, implies materialization of the double and teleportation. There are, in fact, many reports of other bilocating saints, for example, the remarkable cases of Saint Martin of Porres and Sister Maria Agreda of Spain.[110]

The Padre was, on many occasions, said to disappear from the confessional, a structure in full view and always surrounded by crowds of devotees. He would then reappear in the rectory or sacristy. Asked about these disappearances, which he said occurred when he was unable to breathe, Padre would casually reply, "I flew over your heads."

One type of bilocation Pio was apparently capable of involved his characteristic odor. The odor of sanctity is linked with the phenomenon of bodily incorruption. The incorrupt bodies of saints are known for their surprising fragrances. By means of paranormal fragrance, Pio made his presence known to people at a distance. The scent emanated from his person and also from the blood that came from his stigmata. The first doctors who examined him complained that the monk was using perfume. Padre Pio's brand of "perfume" was noticed by people far away from him, sometimes thousands of miles.

Bernard Ruffin, whose book on Pio I highly recommend,[111]gives a detailed account of the fragrance occurring to a Lutheran seminarian, Robert Hopcke, in Plainfield, New Jersey, in 1978, ten years after Pio's death. William Carrigan, normally skeptical of miracle stories, reported to Ruffin his perception of the aroma at his desk at Foggia (about 20 miles from the monastery): "I had no trouble in identifying the aroma as that of Padre Pio. It wasn't something you could confuse with any other odor." Padre Alberto D'Apolito, Pio's confrere for many years, wrote in 1978: "The reality is that hundreds of thousands of individuals, even unbelievers, have testified and continue to testify that they have suddenly and inexplicably perceived the perfume of Padre Pio." Many non-Catholics report having sensed Padre Pio's paranormal fragrance. Emilio Servadio, a Jew and leading Roman psychoanalyst, had a powerful experience of Pio's scent during a visit to San Giovanni in 1937.

If the Padre had a knack for "prolonging his personality"[112]in space, he could also prolong it in time. Precognition, if a fact of nature, upsets our normal view of time and of cause and effect. It seems impossible for something that hasn't occurred to influence anything. Even so, many claims of Pio's paranormal forays into the future had been made. These were usually done offhandedly, never as public pronouncements. Pio was unusually prescient about what Italian cities would be bombed during the Second World War and which soldiers would return from the war.

Like spiritual masters in other traditions, Pio foretold the year of his death. And he often had prevision of others' deaths. A young priest, Father Dionisio, on his way to Venice for studies, said goodbye to Pio. "Studies! Studies!" Pio muttered, "think of death, instead, so that when it comes.... " His voice trailed off. A confrere who overheard commented on Pio's strange way of saying goodbye. Pio shrugged wistfully. Twenty days later the young priest was dead.

I once watched a Vatican official on TV say that Pio had told a Polish Cardinal named John Paul he would one day be Pope; he also said the Polish Pope would be brought down in blood early in his tenure. In 1981 Pope John Paul was almost assassinated in St. Peter's Square. Fortunately, he was able to recover from his injuries. I hope Pio's prophetic gift is flawed, for he once said a war was coming that would destroy two thirds of humanity.

Symbolic Transformation of Physical Reality

Do supernormal psychic phenomena reflect an evolutionary trend toward increasing porousness of matter to the goals of consciousness? It sometimes appears as if something were struggling to make matter plastic and permeable to human aims and dreams, especially the matter of the human body.

Eastern, occult, and Christian traditions refer to subtle, astral, pneumatic, and light bodies. The physical phenomena of mysticism reflect this trend toward the symbolic transformation of the body: incorruption, luminosity, inedia, the odor of sanctity, levitation, bilocation, and so on. The stigmata illustrate the malleability of the human body and the power of spiritual imagination. Francis of Assisi was the first to reproduce the wounds of Christ in his own body, and ever since hundreds of cases have been reported. The Church by and large takes a dim view of these lesions, recognizing they may be symptoms of hysteria as much as signs of sanctity.

But Padre Pio's stigmata were unique. Visible for more than 50 years, the apertures in his palms were perfectly circular, and were never inflamed, infected, or suppurated; blood, which issued from all five wounds, was copious and bright red. It effused a preternatural fragrance. At his death the wounds healed without a trace of scar tissue, a fact dermatologically inexplicable.

With Francis and Pio, the wounds arose from prolonged identification with the crucified Christ. Whether we think of the stigmata as miraculous or pathological, they say something about the physical power of mind, spirit—imagination. If imagination can produce such extraordinary lesions, it can be mobilized for healing purposes. With stigmata, life imitates art; both men were first stigmatized while contemplating artworks showing the crucifixion. The stigmatized body is a living sculpture.

Padre Pio's fame is also due to his reputation as a healer. Reports of extraordinary healings continued after his death. Many, if not most, of the healings ascribed to Padre Pio were probably psychosomatic. Intense faith, expectation, contact with an authoritative figure might well lead to improvement in many functional, psychogenic disorders.

But other stories, if true, imply a more unlikely type of healing: Vera Calandra's dying child materializing a new bladder; Gemma di Giorgio's pupil-less blind eyes acquiring sight; and Giovanni Savino's blown out eye (due to a dynamite accident) being rematerialized. So far, however, the medical documentation I've seen for these claims is not altogether compelling.

Claims for medical clairvoyance also exist. In the early 1950s Padre Costantino Capobianco had a sinus problem. X-rays were taken and three doctors recommended surgery. "What are these things?" asked Pio about the X-rays. "They're all wrong." A fourth specialist was consulted; the X-rays were misinterpreted, the surgery would have been unnecessary.[113]

Padre Pio once said his real work would begin after his death. Moreover, the Church requires of her duly canonized saints evidence of postmortem miracles. This seems like a tough requirement, but a possible example may be the case of teacher Alice Jones of Liverpool, England, who suffered from neurofibroma, which paralyzed her from the left hip to the toe. Alice, 50, a Protestant, was visited by a Catholic priest, Eric Fisher, who prayed over her. "As he knelt there," said Alice, "there appeared another figure rising from his body. I was so frightened I couldn't move. The figure had the face of an old man with a white beard. He spread his hands in front of me and I could see the holes in his palms. I seemed to hear the words, 'Stand up and walk.' So I did. And I suddenly felt whole again. Suddenly I was no longer crippled and the man was gone." Later she recognized the face of the man who cured her in a photo of Padre Pio. Dr. Francis Mooney, a Liverpool physician, testified: "I have very often come across neurofibroma and have never heard of a single case where it has cleared up spontaneously. I had her X-rayed. There is no medical explanation for the fact that she is completely cured."[114]

Another item in Pio's supernormal physiology was hyperthermia. Padre Pio produced abnormal amounts of bodily heat. Doctors had to use huge bath thermometers to take his temperature, which often shot up to 125 degrees; the mercury in ordinary thermometers broke the glass. Extreme irregularities in bodily function are well known among shamans and other ascetic types. Teresa Neumann, who had the stigmata and who evidently neither ate nor drank for her last 35 years, is another modern case of an ecstatic plagued and exalted by bizarre bodily symptoms.

In the case of Padre Pio, supernormal heat was related to what was going on inside the man. From his letters and statements, one thing is clear: The Capuchin literally burned with love for Jesus. Young Pio wrote a letter to Padre Benedetto on October 22, 1919, describing what happened to him just before acquiring his fully visible stigmata:

> "I cannot tell you what happened in that moment," he wrote, "which was a moment of sheer martyrdom. On the evening of the 5th, I was hearing a boy's confession [a seminarian at San Giovanni Rotondo] when all of a sudden I saw a most exalted heavenly person. I was plunged into extreme terror. He stood before the eye of my mind, holding some kind of special instrument in his hand, like a very long iron spear with a well-sharpened point. It seemed that fire shot out of its point. Seeing this person and watching him plunge the instrument violently into my soul happened in an instant. I groaned with pain and felt as if I were dying. I told the boy to go away because I felt ill.
>
> "This agony lasted without interruption until the morning of August 7.... It seemed that even my viscera were being pulled out by that spear. Every fiber of my being was consumed by fire."

The heat effects, observed in saints known for their holy ardors, proceed from internal causes; they have nothing to do with normal physical forces. When I spoke with reliable informants at San Giovanni, I was told of even stranger powers the Padre had over physical nature. For instance, Pio had the apparent ability to direct the behavior of animals; in one story, a woman with problems getting up on time for Mass was sent a bird to awaken her and a troop of local stray dogs to escort her to the church on time.

Weather Control

The Gospels tell us that Jesus calmed a storm at sea. There are also contemporary reports of commanding the elements. For instance, the American poet John Neihardt witnessed Black Elk conjure rain from a cloudless afternoon sky "during a season of drought, one of the worst in the memory of the old men."[115] Then we have Jeffrey Mishlove's study of Ted Owens, described at length in *PK Man,* who apparently could cause large scale PK effects like rain and wind storms.

David Barker, an anthropologist, was in Dharamsala, India, on March 10, 1973, when he observed a Tibetan priest-shaman, Gunsang Rinzing, stop a rainstorm to permit a festival of mourning. The shaman had built a large fire and recited with intense concentration mantras for 20 hours. Barker writes: " ...the rain had diminished to a drizzle, and by 10 o'clock it had become only a cold fog over a circle with a radius of about 150 meters. Everywhere else in the area it continued to pour, but the crowd of six thousand refugees was never rained on..." He observed that the atmosphere had an "airless" quality and reports feeling disoriented for weeks after the experience.[116] In light of all this, we have an account of a Roman engineer, Pasquale Todini, who said Padre Pio sent him away from the monastery during a torrential rainstorm but arrived home dry. In the course of the engineer's walk, the rain around him was reduced to a sprinkle.[117] Enough has been said to indicate the range of Padre Pio's curious capacities: special access to internal environments, mastery of time and space, symbolic transformation of physical reality.

Next Step in Human Evolution

My aim in these cullings is to provide examples of phenomena that force us to wonder about who and what we are, and what strange powers we humans may harbor deep within our evolving selves. In these and related anomalies I believe we may be looking at the shape of things to come, images that point to the next quantum leap forward in human evolution.

To be even more specific about my fact-inspired phantasy, I believe we be evolving toward beings comparable to those depicted in ancient literature as Greek gods. In my view, we have enough concrete evidence to imagine this as at least theoretically possible. The Greek gods were immortal and possessed many of the superpowers, mental and physical, that we are tracking. Alfred Russell Wallace, who co-founded with Charles Darwin the modern theory of evolution and was a scientist of unquestioned genius, investigated psychic phenomena, and was, as he said, "beaten by the facts." He therefore sought to build a bridge between psychical research and the theory of evolution.

Wallace was powerfully engaged with Spiritualism, a new offshoot of Christianity based on special experiences that living people were having, detached and separate from the established churches and their dogmatic wisdom and pronouncements. "It would appear then," he wrote in 1878, "that if my argument has any weight, that there is nothing self-contradictory... in the idea of intelligences unrecognizable directly by our senses, and yet capable of acting more or less powerfully on matter."[118] Wallace suggested that some principle of psychic intelligence was needed to round out the approach to the problem of evolution, and emphatically stated that natural selection "is not the all-powerful, all-sufficient, and only cause of the development of organic forms."

But modern biology has followed Darwin and shown no interest in the phenomena that Wallace had taken the trouble to investigate. In my opinion, Wallace laid the groundwork for a more complete evolutionary paradigm. Open to all the crucial data, I mean a paradigm based on the hypothesis of a general intelligence playing some role in evolution, an intelligence transcending space and time, but interactive with nature, and given to what Henri Bergson called "creative evolution."[119] By bringing in the phenomena of Spiritualism, Wallace opened new horizons of thinking about the possibilities of human evolution.

As for future humanity, the ecstasy of the saints, the samadhi of yogis, the Dionysian maenads may hold the secret to our escape from planet Earth, perhaps our entree to navigating the psychospiritual multiverse that we inhabit. The literature of flying saucers shows how frequently levitation is reported. The phenomena take many forms. Gravity-suspending beams of light, for instance, seem to lift individuals into apparent spacecraft. The alien "spaceships" themselves make light of the rules of terrestrial flight dynamics. In the case of Joseph of Copertino, extraordinary levitator, the figure of Mary above in Heaven was the psychic fuel that enabled him to suspend the effects of gravity. In Joseph's futuristic space technology, ecstatic love is the ultimate fuel.

The curious sky epiphanies we call UFOs or UAPs might, for all we know, be dislocated dreams or ecstatic projections of alien visionaries from other worlds. The phenomena of bilocation and levitation may be clues to the secrets of hyperspace travel and the mysteries of UAPs. Other beings elsewhere in the universe are likely to have had millions, if not billions, of years to evolve these crudely and fleetingly manifested capacities of our terrestrial saints and shamans.

The Remover of Obstacles: A Global Miracle

In my next example of something altogether unexpected, the misgiving is not about deliberate deception but mass delusion. This miracle is the opposite of materialization—*dematerialization*. The case was global in proportions. I myself witnessed the phenomenon on CNN. By chance, I saw on my television screen an amazed BBC reporter lift a small cup of milk to a statue of Ganesha, the Hindu elephant God; the milk slowly and clearly diminished and then *disappeared*. Reports of the so-called "milk miracle" began on September 21, 1995, and continued into the next day. Like the Marian visions reported in Fatima and Zeitun, this phenomenon was witnessed by vast numbers of people, and not just in one locale but all over the globe.

Just before dawn a man from New Delhi dreamed that Lord Ganesha, the elephant-headed god of wisdom, wanted milk. The man dashed out to the first temple to make a milk offering to the statue of Ganesha; much to his amazement he watched the milk disappear before his eyes. The impossible nature of what he saw was obvious. Others joined him and witnesses multiplied. By the end of the day, reports of statues "drinking" milk were coming from all parts of India and from Hindu communities in London and other parts of the world. The entire phenomenon, witnessed by millions, seems to have ended after about 24 hours.

"The `milk-miracle' may go down in history as the most important event shared by Hindus of this century, if not in the last millennium," reported *Hinduism Today* in 1996. Ordinary life in New Delhi came to a standstill while liter upon liter of milk vanished into thin air. The stock market in (what was then called) Bombay came to a halt as people rushed to temples to witness and participate in the wonder. Disbelievers sneered and called it "mass hysteria." The initial response of the Indian press condemned the reports as ignorant and superstitious. Newspaper reporters who witnessed the phenomenon from the UK, USA, Denmark, Germany and Canada were less glib. Reporters from the *Washington Post* did not reject as illusion what they personally witnessed at a Maryland Hindu temple. UK reporter Rebecca Maer visited a temple in Southall and wrote in the *Daily Express*, "It's difficult to dismiss something you have seen for yourself." The diehard denier will simply respond by saying that people can be convinced they saw something that was in fact an illusion. True, but proof is needed that it really is an illusion. What I saw on CNN was no illusion. It was perfectly clear; the white liquid, *from inside its container*, slowly diminished in size until it was all gone. Period.

Hinduism Today (January 1996) reviewed roughly 160 milk miracle reports from all over the globe. In contrast to favorable non-Indian reports, they found that the Indian press, based on snap judgments made by "scientists" without recourse to eyewitness testimony, mostly denied there was anything unusual going on. It was assumed, for example, that the milk simply dropped through the drains under which the statues were mounted. That is *not* what I saw with the BBC reporter on CNN. In fact, many statues that "took" the milk had no drains, and one notable Malaysian lawyer's milk offering disappeared by a statue mounted on his car's dashboard!

Desperate theorists claimed that capillaries of the porous stone absorbed the milk and created the illusion of disappearance. This of course doesn't work if you have seen the milk disappear from the spoon or glass. Why, in any case, should this monstrous mass illusion suddenly seize people all over the world and abruptly cease after one day? If there were such mundane causes at work causing the global illusion, why did it suddenly and only occur on that one day?

The irrational denials of the press caused some people who witnessed the event to doubt their own senses. I think the sociology of belief is here almost as interesting as the apparent miracle of dematerialization. Clearly, we see the role of antecedent assumptions shaping our beliefs and perceptions. A great deal about the world remains "invisible," thanks to certain climates of belief, the cultural trance.

With miracles, paradigm blindness can be very intense; it is not an easy thing to overcome. The idea of transcendent dematerialization? That might be unnerving. Still, there were letters from engineers and scientists who observed the phenomena with clear heads. For example, Arpana Chattopadhyays of New Delhi wrote in the *Hindustan Times*: "I am a Senior scientist of the Indian Agriculture Institute of New Delhi. I found my offerings of milk in a temple being mysteriously drunk by the deities. How can the scientists explain the copper snake absorbing the milk I offered with a spoon kept at a good distance from it?"

Disbelievers came up with lame objections. A reporter for the *Indian Express* complained about wasting milk! Others bemoaned the loss of time on the job, so many people having fled their workplaces to witness the wonderfully amusing but superfluous miracle. They complained about the "absence of a scientific temper" without putting the issue to a test themselves. The disbelievers were so frantic they moralized about the "failure of the education system." Miracles, according to Malini Parthasarathy, writing for Chicago's *India Tribune*, were "anachronisms incompatible with the vision of a secular and scientifically oriented India." How rude!—how lower class of miracles! Don't they know their place?

These reports of miracles, according to the official jeremiahs, signaled regression to feudal times. The study made by *Hinduism Today* concluded that the Indian press, in the grips of its modernist bias, ran roughshod over the eyewitness accounts of millions of firsthand experiencers, thus insulting one of India's most popular deities, Lord Ganesha, the Remover of Obstacles.

Two Hindu students of mine were in India at the time of the phenomenon and wrote accounts of what they personally observed. One of them confirmed a fact I had read about in the newspapers. There was a milk shortage around the country as a result of all the milk that Lord Ganesha drank up! Here is the story from my other student, Deepak Bhagchandani: "I have personally witnessed and experienced the opportunity to feed the Lord with my own hands in a temple, in New Delhi. I stood and waited in a queue at the Ganesha temple. It was astonishing and unbelievable when my turn came to offer milk to the Lord. I took a spoonful of milk in my hands and placed it near the sculpture. The milk disappeared slowly and gradually. It was not flowing down or being wasted. As a matter of fact, I could see no traces of milk anywhere." Deepak adds that he returned to the queue three times for a repeat performance. (Deepak also wrote an account of his witnessing "bhabutti," or sacred ash, materialize from a Sai Baba photo, a widely reported phenomenon.) Remarkably, this story of Ganesha, altogether astonishing, quickly vanished from public consciousness; it seems to have made a very slight impression on the Western mind.

That Western mind set in India has blinded Indians from seeing some real metaphysical shockers in their own backyard. A similar repression of the miraculous was at work in the life of Padre Pio. The American clergy, according to Kenneth Woodward, was not sympathetic to the bleeding stigmatist, now St. Pio, who seemed like a throwback to medieval masochism or perhaps Victorian hysteria. According to Ennemond Boniface, in a book published soon after Padre Pio's death, some people inside the Catholic Church plotted to do away with the Padre.[120] They resented him for using his charismatic powers to create an adoring cult, an accusation unsupported by credible testimony.

Reconnoitering Human Capacity

Let's pause now and grant there is a solid mass of empirical fact undergirding our basic story. In the next chapter, I plan to shift to questions about meaning. Kenneth Woodward's *Book of Miracles* explores the meanings of miracles, according to the religions that create or experience them. My search for the meaning of miracles is more general; I see the variety of miraculous phenomena as a precious inheritance of the human species at large. As such they may be viewed from many perspectives: metaphysical, activist, artistic, futuristic, evolutionary. Miracles are data that should be of interest to new paradigm aficionados. The playing field of miraculous powers is open to all, even to individuals turned off by religion and intolerant of its shortcomings. The word *miracle* one might take as code word for powers latent in all human beings that manifest in special and mostly unpredictable conditions—a word that represents a temptation to push matters as far as possible to the edge of something altogether new.

The potential for miraculous power is pervasive, and affects all aspects of experience: mental, physical, biological, even of time and space. Based on numerous observations, the essential mental state, the state conducive to metaphysical breakthrough is *ek-stasis*, ecstasy, "being beside oneself." One has to get out of one's habitual, guarded stance before things. Whether by luck or practice, an ability for total absorption in the object of attention—this seems the link to the psi event. The example of Joseph of Copertino illustrates the link between ecstasy and levitation.

There are different types of miracle. One pattern is about upending physical laws, for example levitation, bilocation, apports (matter through matter), poltergeists, teleportation—all modes of overturning our habitual concepts of space and time. There are miracles of the body, living and dead; among Christians, saintly corpses remain incorrupt, refusing to decompose; among Buddhist saints, dead bodies slowly shrink for about seven days and on the eight vanish into the void, after which the sky is filled with rainbows.

If many miracles revolve around death and after death, a great abundance of healing miracles also exist. There are biological wonders such as inedia, authenticated cases of individuals who live for months or years without eating or drinking, in effect, graduating from normal natural life, stepping into a veritable new mode of being. We seem to be seeing the effects of an unknown agency that transcends familiar nature, and that possesses extraordinary healing power.

Another category of miracles involves making history, as in the prophetic career of Joan of Arc and the voice and paranormal light that changed Paul of Tarsus into a founding apostle of a new religion. People have made history as a result of one or another venture into psychic otherness. The day of Pentecost that the disciples of Jesus heard a roar and were crowned by mysterious tongues of fire has been called the birth of Christianity, the result of a visit from the Holy Spirit, as it was called, or whatever it was.

There are sensory miracles, perhaps the most universal being the experience of divine light in mystical and near-death experiences. Also under sensory miracles we have much evidence for what has been called the odor of sanctity and, less endearing, the odor of devilry.

In recent times we have records of what seem to be examples of *globally distributed miracles*: the visions, healings, and materialization linked to the Virgin Mary and the milk miracles of 1995 associated with statues of the Indian god Ganesha, the Remover of Obstacles.

One-off miracles are also found in our data trove, for example, the account I cited from Edward Gibbon about the Christians of Tipasa whose tongues were ripped out of their mouths but by some not understood process retained the full use of articulate speech, a fact confirmed and recorded by impartial witnesses. The power behind these supernormal manifestations is highly adaptable and opportunistic, at the same time picky and unpredictable.

Four: Things to Do with Miracles

We need to carve a niche for miracles, free from the regimented demands of science and the compulsions of religion. Disengage the concept of miracle from its old-fashioned problems and presumptions, and return to the phenomena themselves. For one thing it should wake us up to knowing what we do not know. But for those with an experimental cast of mind, there are several possible uses of miracles.

A Prophylactic for the Faithful

To begin with, miracles serve as an all-purpose prophylactic against the conceit of scientism.[121] It's not just individuals who suffer from this cognitive malady; whole cultures do, branches of science, theology, and philosophy. Nature is *nothing but* physical, and *everything* in nature obeys the same physical laws. True explanatory principles must be physicalistic, for all things are reducible to physical reality. The idea that a god called Ganesha, Remover of Obstacles, could somehow dematerialize milk has to be a joke. Ditto for the belief that an ecstatic friar like Joseph of Copertino could regularly take off into the air in defiance of gravity. The belief that a religious statue could weep or a painting bleed is of necessity absurd. And so on through the entire list of reported phenomena we've canvassed. According to the conceit of scientism, they just cannot be what they claim to be, which was the whole of Hume's pseudo-argument against miracles.

Thomas Jefferson tried to reduce Christianity to ethical rationalism; it worked very well for him. Jefferson and the rest of the founders were extraordinary but scarcely men of ideal character. The great man's treatment of miracles in the New Testament was biased and superficial, to put it mildly. Miracles are doors to realms of experience that scientific materialism rule out *ex cathedra.* They are useful to believers insofar as they testify to the power of mental attitudes linked to faith—it turns out that there's more to "faith" than mere irrational hope. One of the strongest findings in parapsychology is implied by the "sheep-goat" effect, the fact that belief seems to amplify the occurrence of paranormality. In other words, carefully controlled experimentation in parapsychology supports traditional ideas about the value of belief, faith, and trust. Empirical research also supports the idea of the effectiveness of prayer. So there are grounds for gaining the respect of traditional religious believers.

For Science, a Cornucopia of Anomalies

But now, what about science? *Anomalies* are often harbingers of progress in science. As Thomas Kuhn argued in *The Structure of Scientific Revolutions* (1962), at critical points of history anomalies often serve to trigger revolutionary advances of scientific knowledge. Anomalies are not for the faint of heart, and miracles are among the extremes of anomaly. For the adventurous scientific explorer, however, they furnish a feast of challenges to big assumptions of established science and serve as openings to new realms of experience and experiment.

The anomalous (literally "law-breaking") is a sign that something unknown and perhaps deeply important needs to be investigated. New laws, new forces of nature, may be awaiting discovery and recognition. It seems fair to say that miracles point to facts that restore mind to a central place in the broad scheme of nature.[122] I see no reason to doubt that with the ratification of miracles we add elements of power that might be harnessed to accelerate the creative advance of our species. The extraordinary phenomena should be taken as signs of human evolutionary capacities. There is no reason to suppose that further evolution of our species, mental and physical, is impossible or unlikely. Certainly, there is plenty of room to evolve into more fully evolved versions of our species self. Some pessimists about our human future might consider launching a project to jump-start the psychophysical evolution of our species.

In the prophetic tradition, signs and anomalies are associated with breakthrough to new modes of being. I believe that the events we're tracking called miracles may foreshadow a general transformation yet to come. Science from that viewpoint would need to assume the mantle of evolutionary activism. In *that* progressive light, miracles should be an inspiration to the advance of human consciousness. Many today are searching for a new science of spirituality. In my view, it would be a science based on human experience; a science that affirms as fundamental mind and consciousness: boundless, irreducible, nonlocal, and radically creative. Miracles would be the bedrock of spiritual explorers who were animated by the great spirit of science. All this qualifies as the appeal to science.

Surrealist Performance

We are pondering possible uses of miracles in our age of disbelief and mounting existential angst. Religion and science have things of value to gain from this strange cohort of facts and probabilities. Miracles, however, also speak to the world of the arts, at the least serving as subject matter for representing in imagery the events in question. The images in a way sometimes lead back to the source of the miracle itself, as when statues weep or bleed or milk dematerializes. The idea of using art, not only to memorialize miracles of the past, but to create new miracles—that would be a step forward.

For example, miracles have an affinity for Surrealism.[123] The French investigators of the Medjugorje visionaries described the experience of the Virgin Mary as superimposed on the visionaries, in a relationship they called *surreal*. Laurentin and Joyeux described the Marian visions as emerging from a world that *contains this world*. The temporary merging of the two worlds of experience are like a surrealist merging of dream and reality. The surreal, as Andre Breton the principal theorist of Surrealism saw it, is made by the subliminal mind blending with the rational world; dream, in short, merging with waking reality. Breton read the English psychical researchers, especially Frederic Myers, and he read Freud, which led him to experiment with automatic writing and drawing.

The object is to enter surreal states of mind and create surreal art objects; the first step is to yield to the spontaneous flow of thought and imagery, but the ultimate aim is to incarnate in one space the perfect blend of dream and reality. Breton wrote: "I believe in the future resolution of two states (in appearance so contradictory), dream and reality, into a sort of absolute reality: Surreality."[124] I know of few more daring and ingenious proposals for a school of artistic practice. For Breton Surrealism had a political as well as a metaphysical dimension. To bring dream and reality together must be an all-embracing enterprise that touches on politics, everyday life and love, art and metaphysics.

The levitations of St. Joseph have earmarks of a surrealist performance. Everything that Joseph does in his state of ecstasy—float in the air, be immune to fire, feel no pain, not be distracted by the din of the external world—was something that in principle we can all do while immersed in dream space. The difference is that the observers of his levitation were awake. Joseph's dream reality becomes temporarily fused with the space of the waking world around him, and so fits Breton's definition of a surrealist performance.[125] It does seem that the phenomena we call miraculous are phenomena we might experience in dreams, but more vividly spilling over into our waking world.

The surreal imagery of the miracle points to another existence, a region of human experience far from what Hume called the "customary conjunction of events." From a Humean perspective, "reality" is nothing but the experience of physical impressions in their customary conjoinings. Hume is rigidly committed to the massive *uniformities* of experience,[126] so that Joseph's ecstatic levitations are of necessity intolerable.

There is another kind of surrealistic revolution of the psyche, ready to break from expectations of what is customary. Surrealism specializes in incongruous juxtapositions, the sudden intrusion of the irregular and the exceptional. Surrealist painter Max Ernst defined collage as the "systematic exploitation of an accidental or deliberate meeting of two unrelated realities on a plane that is related to neither—and the spark of poetry that is kindled by the coming together of these realities."[127] Complete openness to the *uncustomary* conjunction of events is the breeding ground of poetry and miracle—a word to the wise, if we hope, as William Blake said, to "live by miracle."

The quest of the poet Paul Roux, a hero of Breton's, brings this into relief. Roux, murdered in his fairytale chateau by the Nazis in 1940, had renamed himself Saint-Pol-Roux, and redefined poetry as the way to a new revelation. It was a surrealist meme that poetry should be made by all. Through the alchemy of the word, and the magic of ordinary phenomena that surround us, it is possible for "humanity to be the architect of its own paradise." All the arts will one day unite under the one banner of this aim. Heaven will unite with Earth, flesh with dream. Time and space will become elastic and matter tamed by sacred powers. It is our duty, said this martyr, to "sur-create," to "claim for one's own time the distant promises of religions."[128] With that haunting claim, the poet reclaims miraculous power from the prophet.

The word of the poet, liberated from the logic of prosaic life, becomes a source of true hallucinations, an evoker and multiplier of meanings, and by means of it, we will learn to love, as Aragon, the surrealist poet, said, "the daily miracle" of existence. Miracles, then, with their totally unexpected juxtapositions, are appropriated from traditional revelation and used to transform the trivia of everyday life into sacred encounter.

The links we have traced between surrealism and miracles point to the core obsession: not, are there miracles, but how can I live by miracle? Saint-Pol-Roux sought the hallucinatory power of words as his way of living by miracle while Breton was learning from Richet, Flournoy, and Myers the methods of mediumship and automatism. In modeling the future human, we want to bring the poet, understood as the maker, back to the center of the great project of conscious evolution. We are pondering the various uses of miracles, ways we can use them in everyday life as well as life beyond the everyday. Religion, science, and art, all stand to gain from recovering the miraculous dimension.

Freedom from Limits Arbitrarily Imposed on Experience

Just *how* we can use miracles is a bit subtler. At any moment we experience as much of the world that our ideas, senses, and assumptions permit; the rest remains invisible, or shrouded in vagueness and generalities. Education to life itself is an endless chain of negations and inhibitions, with fear always a close companion. All this we have to endure through the psychically shaded lens of our worldview; colored by the dominant power structures, oriented to constrain and channel what we can think and feel.

Religion is historically shaped in such a way that it invalidates wide realms of experience as sinful, taboo, morally suspect, damnable, or diabolical. Likewise, science, as the self-appointed vanguard explorer of the universe, has erected its own set of barriers against the free exploration of experience, prematurely categorizing what is invalid, impossible, and reactionary. Constraints on the exploration of existence are normal for historically ossified paradigms.

The human condition is hemmed in by outer and inner constraints; nevertheless, transcendence is always happening. The extraordinary incidents we have described are examples and harbingers of things greater yet to come. The foray into miracles should remind us to resist the arbitrary restriction of what we imagine as possible. Against the specter of all forms of totalitarianism, miracles are signs of the revolutionary freedom of the possible, which sporadically erupt into life, often at critical moments of personal and even world history. Miracles suggest that we always be ready for the impossible.

Five: Living by Miracle

As to Myself, about whom you are so kindly interested, I live by Miracle.

William Blake

To believe your own thought, to believe that what is true for you in your private heart is true for all men—that is genius."

R. W. Emerson, *Self-Reliance*

The question itself has the ring of anomaly. How does one "live by miracle"? Is there perhaps an affective, a cognitive, an existential style that opens the way to sparking the breakthroughs in life we call miracles? What indeed would it mean concretely to *live by miracle*?

For the poet William Blake miracle had much to do with creative imagination. "Imagination is eternity," as he put it, the ultimate reality, the creative mind. Words like Blake's have a ring of mystery, but what do they mean? Where can they take us? What would it feel like to live, move, and have our being from inside a miracle-conducive world? I'm of the opinion that we have to follow our own path to become decently evolved individuals. Fortunately, however, we have forerunners, along with a thing called history to consult with for possible guidance. In reviewing the miracle-makers, I've racked up four points for a model of how to "live by miracle."

The Variable That Moves Mountains

One sturdy result of parapsychology underscores the miracle-conducive power of belief. Belief, however, not *doxa,* which refers to one's creed, but *pistis*, which means trust. Belief, trust, and expectation are among the elements that shape our paranormal IQ. What the evidence overall shows is that those who *believe* in psychic powers seem more likely to have psychic experiences; whereas disbelievers miss the target to an extra chance degree. The evidence proves that disbelief can make you proficient at *negative psychic function*. One wonders if strong disbelievers produce negative miracles. We might not want one for a business partner, a neighbor, or a spouse. The so-called "psi-missing" effect in parapsychology suggests it is wise to avoid the company of the unlucky.[129] Some unfortunate souls just seem like born "losers," folks with a talent for "psi-missing."

We seem to bias our chances for or against a miracle according to *how we feel what is possible at a given moment*. It is one thing to accept in the abstract that something is possible, but it's quite another to feel and be confident at a particular moment that it will occur. Given the relationship between attitude and outcome, can we place ourselves in a miracle-conducive frame of mind? We have the right to form our own belief-system and test it against experience. Why not then explore the life-transforming benefits of mystical and paranormal experience?

One German philosopher was so impressed by the creative power of belief that he argued for the practice of living—thinking and acting—*as if* the world were such and such.[130] Suppose we were uncertain about choosing values or attitudes–say, trust *or* suspicion, compassion *or* indifference, courage *or* fear, and so on—then lived, thought, and acted *as if* one or the other were the truth. Different attitudes, different "as if" scenarios, would result in different lived outcomes. And so, in fact, we might "create" our own picture of the world as we go through time and life.

In 1922, a German philosopher, Hans Vaihinger (1852-1933), published an extraordinary book about the creative power of fiction: *The Philosophy of As-If: A System of the Theoretical, Practical, and Religious Fictions of Mankind*. This philosophy of "as if" is a form of philosophy suited to individuals with an experimental cast of mind.

It is, as I see it, an approach that partners with art as much as it might with science. The "as if" experimental approach can generate new experiences and cause the hidden aspects of ourselves to come to the fore. A new view or attitude becomes an agent of transformation. We adopt alternative views; we test and tinker with them *as if* they were true, and see what, if anything, results. Vaihinger's idea gains power once we bring in the arsenal of supernormal data. Evidence underscores the fact that our beliefs, attitudes, and expectations can be decisive in shaping possible paranormal experience.

In *The Decay of Lying*, the Irish poet and playwright Oscar Wilde lamented the literal-mindedness of the rising culture around him and feared the inventive spirit was being killed by inappropriate fact-mongering. Wilde, like Vaihinger, would say to those who would "live by miracle": do not permit yourself to be hypnotized by the prevailing truths and assumptions of the day. Every age, locale, and culture is dominated by accidental worldviews and fashionable ideas. The challenge to those who would "live by miracle" is to break from the archetypes of authority that keep our highest potentials locked down and inactive.

Life as performance art requires that we practice with "counter-factuals," in other words, step beyond our boilerplate responses to reality and join the fight against imagination decay. Psychical researcher Kenneth Batcheldor found that belief—serene, nonchalant, yet absolutely confident expectation—was conducive to the levitation of physical objects. According to Batcheldor, hesitations, or qualifications, due to fear or rational scruples, hinder the supernormal outcomes. Undue emotion that strains or declaims is equally fatal to success. There is an Italian notion, *sprezzatura*, "nonchalance," a kind of alert relaxation, a calm intensity. Incapacity for paradox will also destroy the effect. Equally fatal, it seems, is solemnity. During experiments, Batcheldor encouraged a party atmosphere, and participants sang, laughed, and behaved with self-aware abandon.[131]

Jesus had the chutzpah to say that faith could move mountains. And indeed, nobody knows the limits of psychokinesis; Batcheldor thought it was limited by fear and expectation. We know the story of *Peter:*

> "Lord, if it is you, command me to come to you on the water." He said, "Come." So Peter got out of the boat and walked on the water and came to Jesus. But when he saw the wind, he was afraid, and beginning to sink he cried out, "Lord, save me." Jesus immediately reached out his hand and took hold of him, saying to him, "O you of little faith, why did you doubt?" (Matthew 14:28-33)

Everything depends on maintaining a certain state of mind, cultivating what Batcheldor called a "special skill." Peter had it but depended on the presence of Jesus, as Lord Adare enjoyed immunity to fire only in the presence of D.D. Home. Peter succumbed to fear of the wind and lost whatever it was that kept him immune from gravitation. "If the sun and moon should doubt," said William Blake in *Auguries of Innocence*, "they'd immediately go out."[132] Blake, like Jesus, a master of hyperbole, makes the point in the most extreme way.

The variable that moves mountains is cited in the Lord's prayer: "Thy will be done." A miracle-conducive lifestyle would seem to be based on trustful surrender to divine providence. This is a difficult concept for rationalists and egotists to deal with. But surrender to a "higher" power can in certain contexts be the liberating thing to do, as described by Jean Pierre Caussade in his *Abandonment to Divine Providence*.[133] The more I imagine that the outcome depends exclusively on me, the more it seems that I'm inwardly ill at ease. I have to hone my creative lying, get better at seeing the world "as if" it were something that draws me onward. A high point is achieved when you believe that whatever happens to you, including the bad, is for your final gain, even if at the moment you fail to see the boon in your misery. It's the hardest role to perform, staying up in spirit when you're down in fact. So we are told by this French master. Whatever happens in the course of daily life is part of God's secret plan for our ultimate well-being; a stroke of genius, as far as practicing the philosophy of "as if."

A Christian writer, a German philosopher, an Irish wit and poet, an English psychical researcher—there is convergence on the creative value of faith, trust, confidence, believing, make-believing, imagining, acting-as-if, and so forth. All involve active modes of consciousness, active imagination, all refusing to be paralyzed by the obvious or impeded by a feckless rationality. So there we have it, students of miracle-making: step one toward a miracle-conducive life-style. Believe and live to the hilt!

The Need for Introversion

If you seek the truth, said Saint Augustine, "go within." Psychical research is equally emphatic about the importance of "going within." Internally focused states of mind such as dreaming, hypnosis, meditation, inspiration, near-death, psychedelic, and even psychotic ideation sometimes elicit impressive psychic and spiritual phenomena.

When we focus inwardly we notice things that otherwise escape us, as when a house is very quiet we may hear all manner of creaks, drips, and knockings otherwise masked by the day's noise level. The challenge is how to remove the blinders from normal perceptual life. One thing seems clear: reduce the noise of the internal *and* the external world and you increase the probability of detecting signals from the deeper regions of our mental environment—which is, as Heraclitus said, "boundless."

Yoga, according to Patanjali, aims to achieve *samyama*, a controlled single focus and stilling of the mind. A large part of his classic yoga manual describes a stunning array of *siddhis* or miraculous powers said to result from the extensive practice of *samyama*. According to the formidable Dr. Rammurti Mishra, "by development and application of *samyama*, discoveries about mental life which revolutionize the entire sphere of human psychology and philosophy become possible."[134] The *Yoga Sutras* of Patanjali inspired parapsychologist Charles Honorton's thinking on the relationship between internal attention and psychic experiences. Parapsychology supports Patanjali's claim that introverted states of consciousness give rise to *siddhis*—paranormal psychic attainments. Honorton wrote of "the relationship between successful psi functioning and…attention toward internal processes such as thoughts, feelings, and images."[135] Modern consciousness research and Christian mysticism and charisms are also consistent with Patanjali's Yoga Sutras.[136]

With regard to living by miracle, one idea often turns up. Extreme ascetic practices seem associated with psychophysical effects we call miracles. The connection between torturing the body and transforming the body was evident from my study of multi-miracle man, Joseph of Copertino. Kenneth Woodward is right when he says "the fact remains that extreme asceticism was identified everywhere in the ancient world with the acquirement of supernatural powers."[137] What he doesn't do is ask why that is so. What do ascetic practices have to do with supernatural powers?

The most radical form of introversion is forced upon us through sleep. Sleep is introverted in two ways. During REM sleep, and the intermediate hypnopompic and hypnogogic states, the waking world is still present but is transposed in fantastic fashion. There is another dimension of introvertive sleep that is dreamless and totally non-conscious. Various things may be said about this form of introversion; it is the most refreshing kind of sleep, but there is a mystery as to why the organism is revitalized by these periodic episodes in which consciousness seems temporarily extinguished. It is another case of an obvious psychological attribute that is without any established mainstream explanation; other examples, to repeat, are memory, dreams, the unity of the sense of self, and of course, the knock out miracle of them all, consciousness itself. The question of what happens to consciousness when it disappears as we enter dreamless sleep seems impossible to answer.

The shift toward internal states opens the way to the greater mind; the problem is how to lower the threshold and access the hidden layers of mental life and learn to use them constructively. Tantric yogic psychologists speak of a "revulsion of the prop," a curious expression for heroic introversion, stanching the outward flow of attention and the inward flow of distractions. Parapsychological findings echo ancient wisdom: trust and internal attention states favor the occurrence of events often construed as miraculous.

Telic Thinking and Miracle-Making

Let's move on from the conditions that lend themselves to extrasensory perception, to conditions that lend themselves to paranormal action, namely psychokinesis (PK), aka telekinesis. It would help if we understood how PK works. But we don't, really. One useful suggestion comes from physicist Helmut Schmidt. In his PK experiments with random event generators, the level of machine complexity made no difference to scoring patterns; psychokinetic ability was unaffected by the complexity of a given task. It is as easy to influence the output of a highly complex machine as it is to influence the movements of tumbling dice.

Schmidt's idea was in essence this: You don't try to influence the mechanism that produces the outcome; you concentrate exclusively on the outcome itself. *What* you are aiming for is more important than dwelling on *how* to obtain what you're aiming for. This is evident in the religious context of prayer. Thinking about the how creates obstacles, implies choice, stress, uncertainty; asking, aiming for the end-result, is a simple gesture. All you do is ask that the sick person heal, that the hungry person get food, that the parties at war become peaceful. You see them victorious, already there, fulfilled.

Schmidt concluded that psychokinesis is a goal-oriented process—a type of teleological or (more briefly) telic causation. "In most of the reported tests with complex electronic equipment," he writes, "the subjects did not know the internal structure of the test machine. They succeeded just by concentrating on the final outcome as indicated by the display device."[138] The modern scientific worldview looks askance at this type of causal influence, and thinks of it as *magic*, linking teleology with magical thinking in a pejorative sense. But this looking down one's nose at "magic" betrays an ignorance of anthropology.[139] What is called magic is usually some form of psychokinesis, so if there is PK, there is also magic.

Psychokinesis, says Schmidt, is a process "*that aims successfully at a final event, no matter how intricate the intermediate steps*" (italics added). One can see how the God idea might evolve in light of our latent psychokinetic potentials; if I believe in God, I can leave it to God to produce my desired outcomes. In fact, to believe in God presupposes a willingness to surrender my finite self to a "higher power," and with God all things are possible. *Let go, let God,* is the old saying. Did the God-idea emerge into consciousness as a way to facilitate psychokinesis?

Jung said that we need to acknowledge our weakness if we hope to mobilize the energies of the creative unconscious. If Schmidt is right about the goal-oriented character of psychokinesis, it opens the door to a forgotten form of thinking, a type of real or natural magic, of using our various mental powers to telekinetically reform reality. (Parapsychologist Dean Radin's book on "real magic" also revives ancient ideas about natural magic and connects them with psychokinesis.[140]) Since our own minds are inherently psychokinetic, it is in our own minds that the link to magic comes to life.

Galileo's new science of mechanics was supposed to mean the triumph of mechanics over teleology. Now we are told by Helmut Schmidt that immaterial thought of a final outcome can bias the course of physical events toward realizing that outcome. Before Schmidt, the English physicist Sir William Crookes, after experiments with D.D. Home, famed physical medium, concluded he had scientifically proven the existence of a "new force" in nature, what today we call psychokinesis or telekinesis.

This sort of telic or teleological thinking has implications for everyday life. The huge popular success of the idea of a "purpose-driven" life draws on our latent capacity for telic or goal-oriented (and to be impish) *magical* thinking. There is a way we might apply this to everyday life by getting clear on our priorities and spending more time marshalling our inner forces on behalf of our specific chosen goals. Otherwise the energies of our consciousness dribble into ineffectiveness. We lose the thread of what we really care for. We get lost in all the alluring possibilities. But context is crucial, so I want to keep repeating: in our techno-consumerist society, it's hard to own ourselves, hard to hold to our goals. It is, after all, a world designed to distract us from ourselves for the sake of interests that have nothing to do with us.

Other cultures have more respect for the soul. Telic thinking, for example, drove native American Papago Indian song magic, which was all about the needs of the soul. Anthropologist Ruth Murray Underhill studied the Papago tribes of Arizona in the 1930s and found a peaceful people for whom song and poetry were a seamless part of life. Underhill observed that the whole style and rhythm of thought of the Papagos differed from modern consumer civilization. Songs designed to enhance the quality of life were repeated on all important occasions: at a drinking party, preparing to make love, during illness or bad weather—every facet of life was an occasion for song magic. "All that is necessary to make their magic prevail is a description of the desired thing."[141] This is Schmidt's goal-oriented thinking applied to everyday life.

Here is the song of a hunter: "I am whistling. Lo! I have found the deer. I am whistling. I am running and shouting. Lo! I have killed the deer." The song describes the desired event, the end-state, the outcome. The hunter remains alert; when the deer presents itself, he acts and takes the deer out.

Schmidt says that PK is a goal-oriented process. Note how Ruth Underhill describes the way native Papago Indians do their song magic: "The describing of a desired event in the magic of beautiful speech was to them the means by which to make that event take place." The singing involved the group and had to be done mindfully at the right time and in the right place. The Papago Indians were of Aztec lineage and a peaceful tribe that yielded pliably to their invaders. They had for centuries adapted to the Southern Arizona heat, barrenness, and constant need for rain. The people were known for their soft-spokenness, their deliberate manner of comporting themselves, and for their disposition to gentle laughter. It was part of their way of singing the future.

It was also part of their way of singing the present. As Underhill writes: "But song was not simply self-expression. It was a magic that called upon the powers of Nature and constrained them to do man's will. People sang in trouble, in danger, to cure the sick, to confound their enemies, and to make the crops grow. They sang as they fought and as they worked, all together."[142]

Modern science banished telic causation from physics and biology. The mechanical replaced "final" causation, and the universe has come to look more like a machine devoid of mind and spirit. Since the 17th century, Galileo's mechanics, not Dante's divine love, reigns over our vision of nature. In the 19th century, it was determined that natural selection was the mechanism of evolution. The meme "survival of the fittest" served to rationalize the morality of modern capitalism that has led to a climate crisis and economic inequity, the combination of which threatens to bring down world civilization.[143]

No wonder there are calls for a new paradigm of living society on Earth—a new way of life that respects the body of Mother Earth and the souls of all the living inhabitants. There is an uprising of a spiritual nature, convergence toward a new philosophy that celebrates an ecumenical, universal oneness of mind. It is a call to unite in new ways, to raise the consciousness of the species.

Testimony confirms that human beings do extraordinary things that fit our definition of miracle. Found in all religions and in all walks of life, miracles are part of human capacity and potential. So, we're asking, what we can do to bring the miraculous mode of thought and being to life?

Granted there is something called telic thinking—something magical, psychokinetic—but what are we to make of it? According to British psychologist Robert Thouless, a condition of "effortless intention" favors the occurrence of these incidents we call paranormal: "Strong volitional effort is unfavorable to success in psychokinesis." Beware of trying too hard. Grinding your teeth won't help. Thouless distinguishes willing from intention: the former he links to effort, the latter to effortless choice. Effort, the huffing and puffing of the ego, can get in the way; so the formula is—*aim without effort.*

According to Father Jean Baptiste Saint-Jure, "prayer has no need of feeling to be of value. It consists solely in the movement of the will towards God." This is Thouless's "effortless intention" applied to prayer. It is also the transpersonal will of Italian psychiatrist Roberto Assagioli in action. In the Lord's prayer, said daily by untold numbers, we hear: "Thy will be done." A perfect example of the release from unnecessary, self-defeating effort. Letting go, releasing effort, relaxing one's grip on things in general—such an attitude may be hard to sustain; but there are times when it can be a life-saver.

The English psychologist Edmund Gurney, who was interested in telepathy and hypnotism, recounts a case of putting a subject to sleep at a distance. It didn't work unless the hypnotizer concentrated on the desired effect—the goal, the end-state. He pictured the desired outcome and focused attention there; that's how he succeeded in putting Monsieur Gibert and Madam B. to sleep at a distance.[144] It's a fine example of goal-oriented thinking by dwelling on the desired outcome. On the other hand, this could be a dangerous talent if one possessed it to an extensive degree.

A text from the Chandogya Upanishad expresses the power of telic thinking: "A man above all is his will. As is his will in this life, so does he become when he parts from it. Therefore should his will be fixed upon attaining Brahman." One needs to consciously aim for enlightenment before the process of enlightenment can begin to unfold in us. In other words, even if the will languishes, one may still have the intention.

A story in *The Little Flowers of St. Francis* illustrates the idea of leading a goal-directed life. Francis and Brother Masseo, happy troubadours devoted to Lady Poverty, were roving the hills of Tuscany when they came to a fork in the road. Brother Masseo got flustered and anxiously asked: "Which way shall we go?" But the master ecstatic from Assisi had a cure for this lapse into needless angst.

Francis directs Masseo to spin himself around like a top, faster and faster, until told to stop. So round and round he goes, "faster, faster," says Francis, until he says "Stop!," and Masseo suddenly stops and drops. Which way is he facing? By chance—it would seem--toward Siena. Now we know which way to go, says Francis to Masseo, and the two men sally forth toward Siena. Coincidentally, they arrive just in time to stop a brawl in which two Sienese young men already had been killed.

The method of Francis accords with the present theory. Masseo was released from the inhibitions of his everyday mind; spinning round, like the ecstatic disciples of Rumi, he lowers the threshold of resistance to the subliminal influx. Masseo lets go of his calculating, linear mind, and leaves things to the intelligence operating below the conscious threshold, what I call the paranormal unconscious. For Francis, to let go is to allow yourself to be touched by the finger of God.

Like 20th century surrealists, Francis of Assisi seems to have striven for a semi-automatic lifestyle—i.e., "inspired." His belief system worked for him, freeing him from self-defeating effort, putting him in touch with a life-transforming spiritual reality. St. Francis was a great spiritual performance artist. One of his gigs was to preach naked to insure the attention if not the conscience of his audience. Several Catholic female ecstatics, perhaps in admiration of Francis of Assisi, are reported to have presented themselves before church statuary stripped naked, involuntary displays of ecstatic surrender to the divine. It was the sort of thing performance artists today might explore as a motif.

Adding teleology provides relief from believing we have to be in control all the time. The Higher Ones (however imagined) have things in hand; no need to torment ourselves with doubt or fear as we move through life. We are pawns in a transcendent game. No matter what happens or what straits we have to negotiate, or what seemingly impossible impasses we have to face, the attitude of "leave it to the Lord" (or something like that) is always an option. If our theory is on the right track, attitude should be beneficial. It should free us from the belief that our resources are ever used up, or hopelessly diminishing, even if it looks like we're at death's door. Something to bear in mind, if you want to live by miracle: connecting with something beyond yourself is pretty basic.

Spontaneity: Lubricating the Miraculous Life

Parapsychology is rich in phrases with metaphorical overtones. For example, the expression *decline effect*, which says that in a psi test scores tend to decline with time; routine sets in, the novelty and inspiration of the first challenge fades, and scores drop to chance levels. What seems to be lost is spontaneity, the invaluable variable.

We need to escape the routines that coagulate our consciousness and keep us shielded from creative chaos. The resolute seeker must know how to deal with the dragon of the "decline effect," the tendency of minds, hearts, lives to harden, to make of existence a self-contracting *hexis*, a mere habit, beastly hebetude.

Parapsychologist John Palmer concluded from a massive review of the literature that the best predictor of paranormality was *spontaneity*—the opposite of habit, the opposite of the stereotypical.[145] When thinking and behavior become rigid and rule-bound, the probability of psi decreases. Spontaneity, what Myers called "subliminal uprush," is the antidote to the decline-effect.

Cultivating a miracle-conducive life-style? A life of constant rule-bound habit might provide a measure of safety but would in due course become boring unto death. Disenchantment follows from a cognitive style chained to the rationality of productive capitalism. Mind and body are organized and regimented by specific economic and social goals, and the ego-driven competitive spirit is all-consuming. Spare psychic energy available for the free play of consciousness—the key to creativity—*is in short supply.*

If the aim is freedom and spontaneity, dreaming may be the way to go. The Surrealist project of Andre Breton asked: How do we consciously tap into the realities of dream space? Obsessed with fusing dream and reality, the surrealist seeks to create a state of mind, a state in which one is seamlessly *both awake and dreaming*.

Various observed types of phenomena fit Breton's concept of surreality—the superposition of dream space on waking space: for example, poltergeists, ecstatic levitations, instantaneous healings, telekinetic hosts, bilocation, inexplicable fragrances, and so forth.

In dreams we know all these things are possible, but sometimes, it would seem, dream reality spills tangibly, or in form of a fragrance, into waking reality. How is it possible? It seems to require a special state of mind, *ecstasis*, getting entirely out of your normally body-riveted mind. Breton was influenced by F. W. H. Myers, pioneer researcher and theoretician of the potentials of the subliminal mind; Myers was aware of ecstasis as the key to the higher states.[146]Max Weber famously described how modern capitalism, rationalism, and bureaucracy conspire to make for what he called a "disenchanted" world, definitely unfriendly to miracles, and hostile to the attitudes and lifestyles conducive to making miracles. Ecstatics don't blend into rationally controlled, relentlessly surveilled bureaucracies that thrive on predictable uniformities.

In this chapter, we have taken a hint from William Blake and are trying to cobble together some rules of thumb for "living by miracle." The idea presents itself at a time when the world seems to be heading toward some very thrilling form of apocalypse.

To live by miracle needs imagination, the vehicle of spontaneous mental life. Imagination is the organ of the possible and the super-possible; by virtue of it we transcend the tyranny of the given. Without imagination, we're trapped in a world of brute fact, stripped of meaning, and affectless. In Blake's living by miracle, you never know what is enough until you have more than enough, and unlike the rationalist, you think the road of excess takes you on a road toward something Blake called "wisdom."

"The man who never alters his opinion," Blake said, "is like standing water and breeds reptiles of the mind." Openness to the many sides of meaning is a powerful indicator of the spontaneity of Blake's miraculous life, which is simply the life of a fully animated, fully intentional mind.

The medieval mindscape, hospitable to wonders of all stripes, saw meaning everywhere. If the great Italian novelist Umberto Eco is right, the more terrifying the outer world, the greater the need to create meaningful symbols. "Even at its most dreadful," he writes, "nature appeared to the symbolical imagination to be a kind of alphabet through which God spoke to men."[147] To be able to read this alphabet calls for a suspension of the everyday mind, it requires something akin to Jung's "active imagination."

Of what use are miracles? Why pay attention to the deviants, the flamboyant eccentrics of nature? My view is something like this: Miracles break open our general idea of how the world works. They issue invitations to reorient our view of what is possible in our own lives. My reaction to the strange phenomena of nature is welcoming. Let them break open the bottle of our blinkered creeds and timid assumptions.

The venturesome miracle-lover should live fearlessly, ready at all times to welcome the unexpected. The universe is a scene where the new, the unexpected, the unpredictable is sooner or later imminent. If the universe is evolving, miracles are not just likely but inevitable, evident in the phenomena we surveyed. Auden's demand for a miracle is grounded in the history of the universe. The universe itself is a miracle, for it might very well *not* have been. Why not expect, or like Auden, even demand, a miracle? Hence to yield with an open heart and mind to the unheralded, the impossible.

The French poet Charles Baudelaire once said that genius was to recapture the imagination of childhood. Conforming to the rules of rational adulthood may serve our practical needs but ruins our receptivity to things magical and miraculous. Surrealist Pierre Mabille writes in his anthology: "Attaining the marvelous requires that the power and knowledge gradually acquired with age help us to extend and nourish the child's spontaneous thought process, rather than to destroy it."[148] A monumental task! The more we collect the data and reflect on the potentials people harbor within, the greater the importance of education. With the death of the humanities on the horizon,[149] the new ideal of education is the ethos of neo-liberal capitalism. With that to cope with, the outlook for psychospiritual education looks bleak. But all is not lost.

The next two chapters are complementary: built out of the materials we've ranged over, they present a model for how ordinary people of any belief or lack thereof might learn to draw on the collective benefits latent in the deep regions of our mental life. This is a model without ideological or religious baggage. It speaks solely to individual explorers of self-knowledge and self-realization.

Six: The Hypothesis of Mind at Large

Our soul cannot embrace its whole extension, nor its whole essence.

Augustine, *Confessions*, x.8

Forming a Relationship to the Unknown

A review of some of the data (we have only scratched the surface) makes it unlikely that reported miracles are all hoax, illusion, or mere myth. Included are data indicative of high strangeness found in the annals of medicine, anthropology, religious history, mesmerism, contemporary placebo research, near-death studies, and more. Viewed *en masse* this extensive database suggests that unknown capacities are a part of human psychophysical potential. Evidence, I believe, points to the reality of a distinctly "greater mind" that is extraphysical, hyperspatial, and transtemporal. This is a giant leap beyond the mainstream view that tries in vain to reduce mind to so much ineffective byproducts of brain activity.

Once we grant that our personal mental life is nested in a larger, apparently transcendent albeit subliminal sphere of mental life, it becomes conceivable that we learn to interact with this greater mind. Changing history forces us to pose the question in a new way. There was a period dubbed by Karl Jaspers the "Axial Age" (roughly 600 BCE to 200 CE) during which many of the great religions and philosophies of the world were born in Europe, the Near East, and the Far East. They were violent times that gave birth to visions of peace, when cities were ruled by philosopher kings, and societies had lions and lambs lie down together. Humans were in various ways discovering the outer reaches of mental and spiritual life, something we'll dub the Transcendent. The names of deities and other spiritual agents come to mind at once, like God, the Great Spirit, angels and demons, and so on. The Axial Age, whose effects are still unfolding, has been crucial to the history of consciousness. But other periods were no less important, such as the Renaissance, the Protestant Reformation, and the fateful Scientific Revolution. A few centuries after Galileo dropped teleological causation from the new mechanistic physics, Darwin's *Origin of Species* struck another blow against the old way of thinking, rendering the creator God of the Abrahamic traditions if not otiose at least highly suspect; so that by the dawn of the 20th century, Nietzsche's Zarathustra had proclaimed the death of God.

My aim here is more to proclaim the death—or rather the bracketing—of certain troublesome vocabularies. Cloaked in the language of God, angel, prayer, heaven, hell, damnation—and, of course, miracle, such discussions and vocabulary may end by cloaking the ideas and facts behind these loaded words that we want to examine. So I would like to translate such issues of religious experience into the language of consciousness and psychical experience, and to use the empirical phenomena of miracles to reimagine how humans might interact with the Transcendent. A big step is involved in moving from the personal to the transpersonal mind. We must step out of our brain-mediated mind into the atmosphere and dizzying perspectives of transcendent consciousness.

It's *dizzying* because we don't know how to identify what breaks into our world and consciousness in ways that upend normal experience. What was it that saved the artist Benvenuto Cellini from committing suicide in prison? Was it an angel or a telekinetic phantasm initiated by Cellini's subliminal mind? The Virginal epiphanies at Fatima or a deliberately crafted video projected by highly advanced ET technology? Or, as some deep reader of the Bible might suggest, could the agent of this deception be his Satanic majesty himself? The point is this: there is much evidence for many extraordinary phenomena, but we don't how they occur in a very clear way, and we don't know *where* they're coming from—but to say perhaps from some crack in Mind at Large.

The Miracle and Fragility of Consciousness

Given the "heterogeneous" natures of mind and brain, William James admitted that the emergence of consciousness from the brain would seem "miraculous."[150] Moreover, without consciousness, there would be no experience; practically speaking, for humanity the universe would not exist. In that sense, consciousness is the miracle of miracles, the basis of everything we experience, including all possible miracles.

On the other hand, our immediate living consciousness is always changing, always more or less unsteady, if not waffling. The fragility of consciousness is caught by the 17th century English poet Henry Vaughan when he wrote:

> I would I were a stone, or tree,
>   Or flowre by pedigree,
> Or some poor high-way herb, or Spring
>   To flow, or bird to sing!
> Then should I (tyed to one sure state,)
>   All day expect my date;
> But I am sadly loose, and stray
>   A giddy blast each way;
>   O let me not thus range!

"Sadly loose" and straying giddily define ordinary consciousness, which lacks the stability that goes with being a stone, a flower, a flowing brook, or singing bird. It is an instability we can verify with a little introspection. The Jungian poet Thomas Moore wrote: "I spent many years trying to become conscious, but all that effort led merely to self-consciousness, which in turn generated guilt, anxiety, and ambition."[151] Our moods, feelings, and perceptions are constantly vulnerable to change; we crave some "one sure state," as Henry Vaughan put it. One might feel "on top of the world" but abruptly be plunged into despair, anxiety, rage, or terror by a doctor's grim prognosis, a radio report of a tornado coming, the death of a business venture, and on and on.

The French mathematician Blaise Pascal remarked that all the problems of the world arise from our inability to sit still, calmly and self-possessed, for any length of time. My immediate personal consciousness is made of fragile stuff; it is volatile, an unreliable ally, thrown off course by trifles, and deep down rattled and uncertain. Permanent distractibility is the essence of "normal" consciousness. A Buddhist scripture says: "Just as a monkey gamboling in the forest grasps a branch, then lets it go to seize another, so that which is called mind, thought or knowledge, appears and disappears in a perpetual change, day and night."[152] No surprise that human beings long for a solid anchor, a lodestar to orient their life journey. The fickleness and unreliability of personal consciousness prompt us to seek something greater to anchor ourselves more firmly.

The Hypothesis of Mind at Large

The worldwide intuition of a "mind at large" is, I believe, grounded in various kinds of unusual experience people have. The English writer Aldous Huxley used this expression in a book about the psychological effects of mescaline. Huxley tried to explain the changes he experienced during his mescaline intoxication. According to the French philosopher Henri Bergson, the brain is the organ of "attention to life," and is chiefly concerned with the business of bodily survival. Mescaline relaxes that narrow focus and opens the mind to unsuspected ranges of consciousness.

Bergson's theory, writes Huxley, states that

> ...each one of us is potentially Mind at Large. But so far as we are animals, our business is at all costs to survive. To assist us in adapting to our physical needs, Mind at Large has to be funneled through the reducing valve of the brain and nervous system. What comes out at the other end is a measly trickle of the kind of consciousness which will help us stay alive on the surface of this particular planet. . . . Most people, most of the time, know only what comes through the reducing valve and is consecrated as genuinely real by the local language. Certain persons, however, seem to be born with a kind of by-pass that circumvents the reducing valve. In others temporary by-passes may be acquired either spontaneously, or as the result of 'deliberate spiritual exercises,' or through hypnosis, or by drugs.[153]

There are in fact many ways to bypass the constraints on what we are conscious of. Bergson suggested that ". . . if telepathy is a real fact, it is very possible that it is operating at every moment and everywhere, but with too little intensity to be noticed, or else it is operating in the presence of obstacles which neutralize the effect at the same moment that it manifests the effect."[154]

Consciousness in itself has an unbounded range, necessarily narrowed in our perceptions by the absorbing tasks of life. However, upsetting normal brain function *may* open a person's mind to the vast consciousness of mind at large. The ways that can happen vary. Brain traumas or being struck by lightning can do it, in some cases suddenly manifesting talents repressed or masked by normal brain life. Near-death experiences fit Bergson's model well enough; violent brain disruption results in dramatic psychical change. By means of more gradual but persistent techniques, our everyday behaviors and experiences can be modified. We might redeploy attention in meditative practice or fast or ingest psychochemicals, i.e., Huxley's mescaline.

There are known and unknown avenues for inducing contact with the greater mind that facts are forcing us to consider. The first empirical step is telepathy. The term was defined by Frederic Myers as "the communication of impressions of any kind from one mind to another, independently of the recognized channels of sense." Later, he writes: "The conception of telepathy is seen gradually to enlarge and deepen, proving to us at last that the kinship between souls is more fundamental than their separations."[155] Mentally, subliminally, we are all part of one mind but are separated by our bodies.

Myers had much to say about the importance of telepathy. "The worst fear was the fear of spiritual extinction or spiritual solitude; the true security is in the telepathic law," Myers wrote, discussing the idea of "spiritual evolution in the Epilogue of *Human Personality*. Telepathy proves that our minds are connected in ways that our bodies are not and may therefore endure in ways that our bodies will not.

Myers thought that "love is a kind of exalted, but unspecialized telepathy—the simplest and most universal expression of that mutual gravitation or kinship of spirits..." Why is love "unspecialized telepathy"? A "specialized" telepathy would be directed toward some specific item of information such as that someone was ill or was doing or saying something. Telepathy (in Greek) means "feeling at a distance," so by "unspecialized telepathy" Myers is suggesting that in love our feeling for a person is pure, unconditional, unbounded by time and space. To borrow a line from T.S. Eliot's *Four Quartets*, "Love is most nearly itself/When here and now cease to matter." Telepathy occurs more readily between people bonded by common emotions, as when a mother unaccountably senses danger to her offspring, or in cases of "crisis apparitions,"[156] in which a dying person appears to friend or relative at the time of mortal crisis. So telepathy sheds light on creativity, prayer, and love; in each case, revealing the hidden ways we are more deeply interactive and interconnected than we might suspect.

Suppose that a general telepathic openness and mutual accessibility of minds were a fact of nature, thus forming, in effect, one live, active mind. Imagine linking our minds into one mental organism, a psychic metazoan with a life of its own, needs, and aims of its own. This hidden linkage would operate subliminally, below the surface of our individual embodied awareness. As the cells of a living body form an organism with higher functions than any individual cells, we can think of Mind at Large as composed of individual minds that form a whole, a life more than the sum of its cellular components. We may assume that this higher mental organism has its own identity and history. Thanks to telepathy, all the thoughts of Mind at Large are in principle subliminally accessible to all component minds, just as all my personal thoughts are subliminally accessible to my personal mind. The boundary separating thoughts within my mind, and the separation between my mind and other minds, are equally permeable and surmountable—*in principle*, if not in practice or on demand.

The deeper we penetrate our subliminal selves, the deeper we get to Mind at Large. The Greek philosopher Heraclitus wrote: "You would not find out the boundaries of soul, even by travelling along every path: so deep a measure does it have."[157] Ralph Waldo Emerson and the Transcendentalists, influenced by German Idealist philosophers, which hark back to Giordano Bruno and Meister Eckhart, had consonant intuitions, as did Eastern mystics and thinkers, of a world-soul or one mind, a recurrent intuition of the so-called "perennial" philosophy. It says we are all subliminal participants in a greater mental life, as Emerson and Walt Whitman suggested in their writings. Mark Twain believed in what he called "mental telegraphy" and had a telepathic theory of creativity. Many of his "original" ideas came from folks around him, he said, and gave examples from experience. The drift of all this is toward the hidden interwovenness of our mental lives, the reality of something we call the One Mind or Mind at Large.

The hypothesis of Mind at Large makes plausible the practice of prayer, which presupposes linkage of our mental needs to inner resources. The philosopher, H.H. Price, had a theory of petitionary prayer based on the assumption of a "common unconscious," a construct similar to Mind at Large. When we petition for something by prayer, we "broadcast" our wish, need, hope to the "common unconscious." Price gives examples of how this telepathically enriched idea of a common unconscious explains the effectiveness of petitionary prayer.[158] Let's not forget Larry Dossey's panoramic overview of the One Mind and his studies of effective prayer and healing words,[159] all pointing to potentials of benign influence.

In the Epilogue to *Human Personality*, Myers summed up the implications of his work on psychical research. He found that ecstasy was the key altered state most likely to open us to the untried riches of our subliminal selves. Myers underscores his pluralism when he writes: "Yet for each of us is a fit ingress to the Unseen." Indeed, many are the modalities of transcendent contact.

Telepathy is one component of our latent consciousness; it differs from clairvoyance, another latent component. Telepathy is about relationship between minds; clairvoyance is about relationship to physical reality. We may now fit clairvoyance into the hypothesis of Mind at Large. In principle, if each of us is Mind at Large, our minds are in contact with the whole of physical reality, and reports that illustrate the reality of clairvoyance surely exist.[160] Telepathy and clairvoyance extend our cognitive consciousness to the outer limits of mind and matter. Each of us is starting to look like what Plato called a "spectator of all time and existence."

A curious book by William Denton, a professor of geology from Boston, called *The Soul of Things* (1863), documents many experiments making the case for the reality of such wide-ranging clairvoyance. Contemporary evidence for terrestrial clairvoyance is sometimes called "remote viewing," well researched, especially for its military applications.[161] If Bergson's theory is correct, there are in principle no limits to the scope of Mind at Large. The only limits seem to be psychological, the result of conditioning, and are in a way self-imposed. According to experimenter Kenneth Batcheldor, what restricts the range of these extended mental capacities are fears, beliefs, conditionings, and expectations.[162]

Given Batcheldor's assumptions, it might be possible to train groups of people to specialize in psychokinetic experimentation. Perhaps an idea for a science fiction novel would be to train people interested in paranormal group dynamics, creating a Special Forces of Miracle Makers who would be dedicated to waking humanity up to the next phase of its possible evolution.

Extrasensory perception may be thought of as having three dimensions: mental, spatial, and temporal. Given telepathy and clairvoyance, we may now invest the hypothetical Mind at Large with the atemporal factor, a move that we justify in light of evidence, spontaneous and experimental, of precognition and retrocognition.[163] There is a quantity of evidence that supports the reality of this deeply counter-intuitive phenomenon, having myself had several striking episodes of precognition that left me without doubt as to its reality.[164]

Reports of retrocognition are rarer, perhaps because people are more anxious about the future than the past. But pressing the implications, our hypothetical mental entity would now expand to include a powerful outreach toward the future. This "future," however, must be thought of as probable, not absolutely determined. We infer this from the fact that some monitory dreams have been proven factually true but not completely; in some instances, the precognition *enables one to change a probable future*, a fact described as the "intervention paradox." A case reported in the English *Proceedings for Psychical Research* illustrates how a recurrent dream of a carriage crash served as a warning for a woman who escaped by getting off the carriage *as she remembered the dream*.[165] Others who confront precognition draw startling conclusions that are counter-intuitive but philosophically intriguing.[166]

We are trying to weld various supernormal mental functions together under the rubric of the one mind. "Weld" is probably the wrong word; all the functions are inseparable aspects of the one mind, the one consciousness. All is "welded" in oneness, an idea that transcends anything we can imagine or visualize. We are trying to conceptualize a greater mind in which, hypothetically, all our personal minds subsist. So far the hypothesis is based on evidence for extended *cognitive* abilities: telepathy, clairvoyance, precognition, retrocognition.

The next theoretical step is to add to Mind at Large its psychokinetic potential, the physically expressive side of the great mind. Aldous Huxley remarked of psychokinesis: "If a human mind can directly influence matter not merely within, but even outside its body, then a divine mind, immanent in the universe or transcendent, may be presumed to be capable of imposing forms upon a pre-existing chaos of formless matter... "[167] Indeed, the evidence for psychokinesis enable us to form a model of a Mind at Large with physically expressive powers that issue in unexplained healings, levitations, fragrances, light epiphanies, disappearances, and much more.

Our hypothesis, enlarged by psychokinesis, speaks of the power to act, to reform the world via the creative agency of mind. In the miracle anthology chapter, we discussed macro-PK effects that suggest the action of some kind of super-mind. Stories of large-scale PK include the case from David Barker who observed a shaman stop a rainstorm; the mass dematerialization of milk in the presence of statues of Ganesha, the elephant god; the prolonged, and photographed, epiphanies of a goddess light-form of Egyptian provenance at Zeitun in the late 1960s; or finally, the several centuries of well-documented medical miracles reviewed by the medical historian, Jacalyn Duffin.

It is possible that the creative force of PK mingles inconspicuously with our mundane actions, for ill or good, amplifying or muting effects; sometimes masked behind the appearance of coincidences, seeping or bursting through in politics, in the arts, in the sciences; and in the accidents and fortunes of everyday life. It might add some edge to existence to muse on the inner links with minds and forces superior to ours, but with our best interests at heart.

In this model, our everyday minds are one with and contain all the potentials of subliminal mind, mystical and paranormal. All is present in any given moment of experience: a constellation of supernormal powers, waiting to be awakened and activated for the sake of possible creative advance. The obstacles to full awareness are within us and no easy matter to remove. But there are certainly good reasons for expanding our idea of the creative power available to us, in light of the hypothesis of Mind at Large.

The Limits of Mind at Large

However spectacular the conceivable manifestations, the present notion of a psychokinetic Mind at Large is not the deity of Abrahamic faiths, supposedly omniscient, omnipotent, and all-benign. There is no clear evidence of moral perfection or of unlimited power; Mind at Large is not 'perfect' or omnipotent, nothing at all like the perfect God imagined and constructed by traditional prophets and theologians. Nor does the present speculation impute any definite moral attributes to Mind at Large. As far as I can see, the moral content would be no higher and no lower than the moral content and dispositions of the people who participate in the greater mind at large. .

Mind at Large—*a logically possible extrapolation of known data*—is not meant to describe God as traditionally understood: absolute, perfect, unchanging, all good, etc; so it avoids the difficulties of theodicy, which tries to explain why a perfect God allows innocent babies to be killed by earthquakes. The agency of Mind at Large makes no claims to perfection, and cannot be blamed for the atrocities suffered by humanity.

Since Mind at Large is not, as Jung said of God in *Answer to Job*, all-good, we assume it has a disreputable "shadow" side. The Hebrew deity was frank about its shadow side when it acknowledged, "I am a jealous God." A jealous God that likes to wreak havoc on its enemies—an emotionally honest God. The early Hebrew conception of deity is in some ways closer to Mind at Large than the purified notions of deity of more theologically evolved Abrahamic thinkers. The later prophets deepened the conception of deity so as to embrace the universal values of love and justice. In any case, different cultures, at different times, interact with Mind at Large in their own idiosyncratic ways.

The point of this chapter is to show that the varieties of supernormal experience confirm the traditional intuition of the existence of a greater mind—a transpersonal mind. We may assume that our minds are aspects of an all-permeating, transcendent sphere of mind. This opens the possibility of new forms of experience. There is much talk and anxiety about "identity" today, and with good reason, things are falling apart. As it turns out, the entire array of phenomena reviewed here have implications for the question of self-identity. In brief, they expand and deepen our normal perception of personal identity.

We may think of ourselves as part of a subliminal self that is greater, wiser, and stronger our everyday selves. Just being aware of the deeper possible relationship with our unknown self has a power to liberate us. It is a momentous shift in perspective, realizing that part of you lies in a kind of normal latency and oblivion, awaiting the right circumstances to be awakened.

Seven: Dialogue with the Transcendent

> *Thus men forgot that all deities reside in the human breast.*
> William Blake

Now we need to ask: Is it possible to have meaningful dialogue with this presence, this transcendent Mind at Large? For religious believers, the question is a no-brainer, and the answer is "Of course! We do it all the time!" Believers don't need a new psi-based theory to explain how and why it is meaningful to attempt to engage with a transcendent mind or commune with something we might call a deity. However, the faithless, the critical, the doubters, even sworn reductive materialists with partially open minds and a yen to experiment might be willing to test the hypothesis.

Given the idea of an imperfect, minimalist deity, is it a conversable entity or an irrational monster? Can we talk with it? Soften its heart with words of awe and worship? Curry favor from its mysterious ways? Form an intelligent, intimate, soulful relationship?

The hypothesis we've cobbled together of the Great Mind leaves us with many questions. The data don't reveal enough of its inner workings to allow for any grand metaphysical pronouncements. Also, I should stress that the hypothesis of a greater mind is naturalistic and provisional, and does not favor or underwrite any particular religious doctrine or tradition.

The Crucial Premise

William Blake wrote: "Thus men forgot that all deities reside in the human breast." God, the divine principle, is in some sense a reality deeply ingrained within our own being. In the present model, we are treating it as the psychical ground of our being. So the question is: how do we dialogue with this ground of our being we call transcendent? Humans have a history of being proactive in the quest for transcendent contact, of devising ways to pry open the treasure-trove of the inner life.

In exploring how this may come about, Fredric Myers reported an experiment in automatic writing that offered a clue.[168] Myers's paper was the first in a series that can lay claim to the independent discovery of the unconscious.[169] The experimenter was a colleague of Myers, a Mr. A., who trained himself to write *automatically,* a word that means "self-moving."

Automatic writing is nothing esoteric. The common experience of doodling with pencil and paper is a case in point. Here is a minor but clear illustration: I was writing a letter using my keyboard; suddenly I thought of the pineapple I forgot to buy; I look back and see that I wrote "pineapple" instead of a person's name "Penelope," as I intended. I unwittingly gave myself a suggestion and carried out a behavior *without attention or intention*; I had a transient graphic automatism, an intelligent behavior, performed without conscious awareness. This sort of thing I suspect happens to many of us from time to time. But there's more to the story. Some people can learn to write full sentences, paragraphs, even whole books, *automatically*, that is, without relying upon the operations of the conscious mind.

In the famous case of "Patience Worth," a literary persona emerged from a Midwestern housewife, Pearl Curran, during an experiment with the Ouija board. The surprising point about the alter "Patient Worth" is that her books achieved prominence, were acknowledged by critics, and praised in *The New York Times*.[170] The automatist writes, or dictates, without plan, effort, or awareness. The relevant muscles do their work, dissociated from conscious effort and the directing intelligence.

With the help of various devices, the automatism can be facilitated. You can use the planchette, a special board that makes the act of writing easier; another is the Ouija board where a pointer is touched that picks out letters of the alphabet, and can form sentences. Pierre Janet used the so-called "method of distraction" to facilitate automatic writing. The writer reads a newspaper out loud while holding a pencil over paper, poised to write. The method of distraction keeps the conscious mind occupied and frees up the subliminal mind to guide, direct, or, you could say, temporarily "possess" the medium's motor apparatus.

For Myers, automatic writing became the key to exploring the psychology of the subliminal mind. Spiritualists used it in hopes of communicating with departed spirits. Myers' study led to his theory of the subliminal self, i.e., the self normally below-the-threshold-of-awareness. This yielded a greater potential capacity than the Freudian personal unconscious or the Jungian collective unconscious. Automatic writing was used by Myers as a tool for conversing with different "strata" of the self, the modes of thought active below the surface awareness of everyday life.

Some automatists wrote intelligibly, often rapidly, connecting the words in one continuous script, unaware of what they were writing. Only after could the writer begin to understand what was written. Graphic automatisms are also found in sufferers of epileptic seizure and in cases of somnambulism. The writings of somnambulists vary from dreamlike ramblings to instances of impressive creative performance.[171]

Myers wrote of gradations of mental performance, shuttling back and forth between normal, trifling automatisms such as doodling to the abnormal, i.e., epileptiform graphic automatisms, and on to the supernormal automatisms of inspired artists, poets, and prophets. Myers liked to range over examples guided by his ideal of an "evolutive" science of human consciousness. He writes: "We can set no definite limit beforehand to any of the veins of unexplored faculty which crop up at intervals from the subterranean realms of our being." Something as innocent as a doodle may be the germ of a visionary poem or prophetic diatribe. The great Italian film director Federico Fellini, for example, explains (in *Fare un Film*) how many of his major movies grew from impulsive sketches, a few lines, a swath of color. Myers explored sensory and motor automatisms, which he took as evidence for the "stratifications of the psyche," i.e., the *subconscious* layers, regions, the heights and depths of mental life.

Mr. A's Experiment with "Clelia"

Let's looks at Mr. A.'s experiment and his encounter with the mysterious and fickle "Clelia." It began on Easter in 1883 and lasted four days, during which he posed questions to himself and received responses in the form of his own automatic writing. He used a planchette. Mr. A. wrote that he became "seriously interested" on the first day and "puzzled" on the second. On the third day, he wrote, "I seemed to be entering upon entirely novel experiences, half awful and half romantic," while on the last day the "sublime" devolved into the "ridiculous."

The involuntary writing movements were such that they seemed to emanate from "another brain." On the second and third day the answers to Mr. A.'s questions came in the form of anagrams that stymied him at first. "I was so astonished at the apparently independent will and intellect in forming the above anagrams," he wrote, "that for the nonce, I became a complete convert to Spiritualism." Suddenly, Mr. A. found himself at least entertaining the belief in life after death. The intelligence appeared to be coming from outside himself.

The planchette on the third day announced the presence of Clelia, a female being who promised to incarnate in six years, which excited Mr. A.'s romantic and mystical imagination. He wrote: "It was evident that I was in communication with a—beautiful?—spirit of romantic name…My snatches of sleep that night were few and far between." On the fourth day, however, the automatic intelligence wrote that Clelia did not exist, although this assertion was also contradicted. The final teasing anagram received was "Wvfs yoitet—testify, vow." Mr. A. writes that "reasoning upon the phenomena has since paralyzed the power of producing them." Mr. A. confirmed the hyperbolical insight of William Blake: "If the sun and moon should doubt/They'd immediately go out."

I want to highlight the effect of this experience on Mr. A. Temporarily, he said, the independent intelligence of the planchette-mediated "writer" converted him to belief in life after death; and he was so stimulated by the mysterious feminine being who promised she would incarnate in six years, he couldn't sleep. This was a very strange experiment, and has drawn comments from several psychologists. Janet, for example, wrote: "The story of the spirit that calls itself Clelia truly forms a psychological document of which one could not exaggerate the importance…Is there anything more curious than this individual who poses questions to himself and who never comes to find there the true solution?" Jung was interested in the Clelia experiment; in his view, when the operator poses a question to the planchette or Ouija board, "Who is speaking?" the effect, he thought, is to bring about a synthesis of a new personality from disorganized elements of the subconscious mind.

For Myers the experiment launched a deep investigation of the human subconscious, what he would call the subliminal mind. Later, he wrote: "But in Clelia we saw produced, for the first time, perhaps, in psycho-physical discussions, an instance of a sane and waking man holding a colloquy, so to speak, with his own dream… (an entity) able to force itself upon the attention of the waking mind."[172] Clelia emerged from A.'s subconscious or subliminal mind, assumed "her" identity, and, via the invention of anagrams and other enigmatic remarks, imposed herself upon and temporarily enchanted the conscious mind of Mr. A.

Myers demonstrates that Mr. A., although slightly inclined to accept Clelia's performance as evidence of an autonomous entity, was in fact (as Mr. A. himself perceived with some disappointment) deceived; Clelia seems to have been an inchoate secondary personality that emerged from the hidden strata of Mr. A.'s mind, a personification of his own dream.

In the next paper of this series, Myers showed that automatic writing can be a vehicle for telepathy. In short, entities of the type called "Clelia" may under some circumstances convey information that originates from *outside the mind and brain of the automatist.* This has implications for a theory of divine entities, e.g., the voices of Joan of Arc. The creation and the powers of "Clelia" furnish a model for understanding how people in dissociated states might receive impressions of higher intelligence and undergo sensations of being invaded by external, supernatural forces. Clelia is a nascent goddess, a bearer of secret wisdom, fascinating and unpredictable. But alas! Also prone to mendacity. She shows us how we can construct a model of a "divine" entity. There is a process at work here: lower the threshold of consciousness; manifest the "secondary" personality, its aura of mystery and transcendent power; and from there, who knows what might conceivably unfold?

Typologies of Transcendent Automatism

In the preamble of psychiatrist Anita Muhl's book on automatic writing, she tells of a 22-year-old woman, weak and recovering from an illness, who was curious about trying automatic writing.[173] Dr. Muhl set up the experiment, and the woman immediately began to write, automatically, without hesitation. As she read a newspaper story of a local murder out loud, her hand wrote clearly and intelligibly on a pad without seeing what she was writing. Her first effort produced "a cunning little fairy tale in rhyme," notes Dr. Muhl. "Voluntarily, she could not rhyme, nor could she make up fairy stories; neither had she the sense of humor exhibited in her writing. When the little fairy story was read to her, she refused at first to believe that she had written it. She had felt no motion in her arm and she had been absorbed in the gruesome details of a sordid crime." What could be more interesting? A witty author peeps out from behind a pedestrian persona.

Consider the remarkable discovery made by the Marquis de Puysegur. A student of Anton Mesmer, the Marquis had put one of his working men into a "mesmeric" trance, and an entirely different personality emerged from Victor, a new Victor, confident, articulate, with the talents of a healer and a clairvoyant. This newly synthesized entity, a higher order personality, spontaneously manifested, quickly forging its own chain of memories and new personal identity.

According to the Marquis, the old (awkward and inept) Victor gradually was absorbed, transcended, and disappeared into the new, involuntarily produced, Victor-persona. This "secondary personality"—the new Victor—eventually became the instructor of the Marquis! In the phenomenon we're discussing, the psychophysical threshold shifts, and a new personality emerges, displacing the old.

Whether for a few seconds, or for days or years, events of this sort show how people might be driven to believe in all manner of strange things that most of us regard as just crazy. It might help to bring in the idea of numinosity, a psychic effect first described by the eminent German theologian Rudolf Otto, a trait he found in powerful experiences of (what he called) "the Holy." According to Otto, it is a force that *fascinates*, or we could say, *mesmerizes* the recipient. Numinosity, according to Otto, is related to the quality of being *ganz andere,* "wholly other." Clearly, Mr. A. was *fascinated* by the "otherness" of the intelligence that confronted him during his dissociated episode.

A dream automatism occurred to me that exhibits a structure similar to Mr. A.'s experience. I had a mild case of gastritis; my doctor urged me to stick to one glass of wine a meal and reduce coffee to a cup a day. I believed that drinking milk would soothe my stomach but the inflammation got worse. Then one night I had a very brief dream: a cameo appearance of a cow suspended in space before me—*a cow trussed up in rope*. The image flashed on me and I was awake. The message was plain enough—quit drinking milk! My dream self-contradicted my waking self. The next day I consulted a nurse at the university where I taught; she confirmed the cow's message, so I quit drinking milk and the gastritis went away.

While in a dissociated mental state, an intelligent source within some region of my mind conveyed a message, coded in a metaphoric image, of practical importance to my health and well-being—a message that ran counter to my conscious beliefs. I may have abstracted this intelligence via cryptomnesia or from the outside world via clairvoyance, or learned of it sometime in the past; nevertheless, something below the threshold of my awareness *took the initiative*, and let me know through a vivid dream symbol that I should stop drinking milk. The involuntary way it appeared gave the impression of something acting on me from outside myself, or at any rate from a remote, unknown part of myself. I think of Socrates and his daimon or Joan of Arc and her voices, and feel that I too may be connected, however weakly or sporadically, to a greater intelligence that has my back. And I think about ways to strengthen the connection.

I cite these mundane narratives to keep our talk grounded in experience. The idea of conversation with a higher, possibly benevolent, intelligence is sometimes foreshadowed by events in our ordinary lives. But we have to notice them and reflect on what they might signify. Most of these experiences probably go unrecorded, though not necessarily unremembered. For an example of a motor automatism that prevented a great artist's suicide, we have the story of Benvenuto Cellini's imprisonment in the Castel Angelo in Rome. Cellini's *Autobiography* tells how in despair he decided to end his life. He had a fractured leg and was wasting away in a dark dungeon, alone with nothing but a Bible and one history book. Here is what he wrote:

> They did not allow me a knife, and so it was no easy matter to commit suicide. I took and propped a wooden pole I found there, in a position like a trap. I meant to make it topple on my head, and it would certainly have dashed my brains out; but when I had arranged the whole machine, and was approaching to put it in motion, just at the moment of setting my hand to it, I was seized by an invisible power that flung me four cubits from the spot, in such a terror that I lay half dead...when I searched my memory to find what could have

> diverted me from that design of suicide, I came to the conclusion that it must have been some divine power and my good guardian angel.[174]

That night Cellini dreamed of "a marvelous being in the form of a most lovely youth" who reproved him for his suicide attempt and inspired him to re-affirm the value of his life. Cellini renounced his intention to commit suicide, regained his health, and eventually his freedom.

The Swiss psychologist Theodore Flournoy called this a "teleological automatism." Cellini, as far as his conscious self could see, was crushed with despair and decided to kill himself. His subliminal self, however, did not agree and took action, so to speak, against his conscious intentions:

> On the one hand we find the motor automatism that seized him at the critical time in a violent muscular explosion, which made him, regardless of his fracture, jump out of the reach of danger. On the other hand, it is subliminal imagination that under the impressive and persuasive aspect of a heavenly messenger, placed before him all the religious and moral arguments which were capable of convincing him and changing his feelings.[175]

Cellini interpreted his motor automatism in religious terms. All we know for sure is that something within Cellini physically prevented him from doing away with himself. For Myers, Cellini had an encounter with his subliminal self, its motor and imaginal components in action. Myers also saw Cellini's experience as one of a type on a spectrum that leads back to Mr. A.'s encounter with Clelia, and forward to yet higher, even more mysterious operations that seem directed from our submerged or, if you prefer, our higher selves.

Socrates' Daemon

To further indicate the scope of the psychical mechanism we're describing, let us consider the death of one of the great men of antiquity. At his trial in 399 BCE, Socrates was accused of importing *kaina daimonia* ("new divinities") by the democratic factions, which eventually led to Socrates' state execution. In fact, the charge was a pretext for revenge; Socrates was sympathetic to certain oligarchs who had recently been ousted from power and was suspicious of the newly installed democracy. The Socratic line was that a democracy short on wisdom eventually succumbs to tyranny. In any case, the philosopher got a raw deal. All members of the new democracy, his accusers resented the old man's constant ironical exposure of their moral and intellectual shortcomings.

Socrates did believe in a "strange god" and said so during his trial, reconstructed for us in Plato's *Apologia*. Throughout his life a *daemon*, a kind of spirit guide, made itself known to Socrates. The main thing it did was to *inhibit* him from doing the wrong thing. It would give a sign indicating danger or warn him about something to avoid. These encounters could be trivial or momentous; nor were they always about himself.

Once the daemon warned his companions not to walk on a certain road; those who failed to take heed were splattered with mud by rampaging pigs. Socrates' daemon was very fastidious. Plutarch's *De Genio Socratis* recounts the story: "Charillus (who ignored Socrates' monition) returned home with legs and clothes all full of mire, so that we all remembered Socrates' familiar spirit with roars of laughter, marvelling how the Divinity had care of him continually." Socrates seems to have had more than a dollop of psychic talent, and like most Greeks of his age, he believed in divination.

Socrates' *daemon* played a key role on the morning of the relentless gadfly's condemnation by the state. The story is told at his trial, and is described in Plato's *Defense*:

> "There has happened to me, O my judges," he said after sentence of death was pronounced, "a wonderful thing. For that accustomed divine intimation in time past came to me very many times, and met me on slight occasions, if I were about to act in some way not aright; but now this fate that you behold has come upon me–this, which a man might deem, and which is considered, the very worst of ills. Yet neither when I left my home this morning was I checked by that accustomed sign; nor when I came up here to the judgment hall, nor in any point in my speech as I spoke. And yet in other speeches of mine the sign has often stopped me mid-sentence. But now it has not hindered me in any deed or word of mine connected with this present business. What shall I suppose is the reason for this? I will tell you. I think it is that what has happened to me is a good thing. And we must have been mistaken when we thought that death was an evil. Herein is a strong proof to me of this; for that accustomed sign would assuredly have checked me, had I been about to do anything that was evil.

Socrates, in harmony with his signaling automatism, felt himself reconciled to, and not frightened by, the prospect of imminent death. This story is testimony to the power of automatisms to shape the life of a man, in this case one of the great philosophers of world history, and to facilitate his dying.

Socrates, inventor of the art of definition and patriarch of reason, was happily attuned to the daemonic guidance of his subliminal self. In this famous lover of wisdom, intellect and intuition enjoyed a fruitful co-existence. In Plato's account, we see a person dying calmly and consciously, in full possession of his reason, but at the same time in accord with his daemonic self. Socrates seems to have been closely guided by a force, an intelligence quite other than his conscious mind. He acknowledged a center of control that came from another place, another stratum of his mind and being. The control exerted itself in minor as well as major matters.

In the case of Socrates, we are face-to-face with an image, an archetype of human integrity. In the *Phaedo,* Socrates puts it paradoxically that he would rather be at war with the whole world than in conflict with himself. Moreover, Socrates, model of the rational mind, was on friendly terms with the daimonic—the subliminal side of himself. Unlike most rational-minded people today, he was fine with the notion of active, ongoing dialogue with some kind of spiritual intelligence.

Joan of Arc

Now consider the case of a world-iconic teenager. This time the psychic invasion—the automatism—appears to exert itself in the field of military action. We know of automatic writing and automatic drawing; in the case of Joan of Arc, we might sensibly talk about *automatic living.* When she was about 12 years old, voices and visions began gently to instruct her concerning how to behave and think, how, in short, to live. They began by prodding her with platitudes: "Go to church." "Be good." But before long her improbable voices sent her on a highly specific and directed mission to the Dauphin, the heir apparent to the French crown; the voices insistently told her to assume the leadership of the French army. The teenager's assignment was to oust the English from France and preside over the coronation of the French king.

Voices and visions guided her to achieve these accomplishments—a dramatic illustration of the power of certain mental automatisms. One might equally think of Mohammed's prophetic inspirations and their enormous historical consequences. The prophet of Islam, who was illiterate, is said to have received the word of God for 23 years through the medium of the Archangel Gabriel. Muslims believe the Koran is a miracle precisely because it was a product of automatic writing, a creation of divine influence. Hitler himself said he went "sleepwalking" through history; but Hitler was no Socrates, no Joan of Arc, no Mohammed. Apparently automatisms need not be moral or benign agencies. Most of them are probably of small significance. Our interest lies in the exceptions—the wild quirks of nature we're calling "miracles."

In speaking of Joan's visions and voices, we take nothing from her, who did all with her wit, courage, and capacity to imagine the impossible. And yet, everything happened as if she were controlled by something outside herself, and which she perceived as divine and supernatural. In the end, Joan lost her life to her enemies. Her story suggests there are forces guiding some of our lives *not for our good but for a greater good.* Myers wrote that extraordinary people like Socrates and Joan of Arc help us imagine what humanity may become, a stage where reason, good will, and intuition all unite in flourishing life.

The experiment with Mr. A. shows how certain "religious" experiences might bring about their effects. Mr. A. communes with the mysterious Clelia, who fascinates and overpowers his imagination. More profound experiences than Mr. A.'s led to more profound and lasting beliefs, as in the stellar examples of Socrates and Joan of Arc. But other than individuals, there are whole domains of human experience, such as the prophetic tradition of the ancient Hebrews and the practice of divination in ancient Greece, are rooted in experiences that overflow from the subliminal mind. They differ in many ways but prophecy and divination are about coping with the contingencies of everyday life.

Hebrew Prophets

The Hebrew prophets injected a powerful ethical impulse into the character of their psychical seizures. The prophet, as a type, is caught up in Myers' "subliminal uprush." A voice, a word, an image, a vision just comes, a center of intelligence that speaks to and in some way is "heard" by the *nabhi*, the prophet. The word *nabhi* means "called."

Called by whom, by what? Scholars distinguish Israelite prophecy from Canaanite cults of sympathetic magic; in magic, the human tries to manipulate the divine. In prophecy, "the initiative rests solely with God."[176] In Numbers Chapter 11, a group of 70 elders were swept away with prophetic ardor: "Moses went out and told the people what Yahweh had said. Then he collected seventy of the people's elders and stationed them round the tent. Yahweh descended in the cloud. He spoke to them and took some of the spirit that was on him and put it on the seventy elders. When the spirit came on them they prophesied – but only once." Moses was not alarmed by this and thought it a good idea for the spirit of Yahweh to descend on the populace with abandon. The story seems to illustrate an episode of psychic contagion, as well as a certain democracy of spirit.

A story in 1 Samuel (19:24) illustrates the involuntary character of the prophetic seizure— about Saul trying to kill David. David fled to Samuel at Ramah for protection, and Saul sent his agents three times after David to capture him. Each time the agents witnessed the "community of prophets prophesying," and each time they themselves "fell into frenzy." Saul got word of this and went to David and Samuel in the huts of Ramah himself. Upon arrival, he too was seized by prophetic rapture: "He too stripped off his clothes and he too fell into a frenzy in Samuel's presence, then collapsed naked on the ground for the rest of that day and all night."

The prophetic performer used flute, harp, and tambourine to bring on the necessary altered states and sometimes used symbolic mimes for effect, as in Jeremiah (19:10): "You must break this jug in front of the men who are with you, and say to them, 'Yahweh Sabaoth says this: I am going to break this people and this city just as one breaks a potter's pot, so that it can never be mended again.'" The narrative underscores the connection between theater, sympathetic magic, and prophetic possession.

Initiation from an external agency is clear from many examples in the Bible (Ex. 3:1-17; Is. 6; Je. 1-4; Ezk. 1-3; Ho.1:2; Am. 7:14;

John 1:1). The prophetic experience itself is sudden. More often than not, the description of the seizure, which is verbal, is simple. "The word of Yahweh came to me, saying…" Sometimes the prophet receives the divine message in a dream, sometimes in a vision. As words *just come* to the prophet, so do visions. Thus, Amos: "This is what Lord Yahweh said: there was a swarm of locusts..." Words come to Amos, though he resists the idea that he is a prophet, then qualifies, "But Yahweh took me as I followed the flock, and Yahweh said to me, 'Go and prophesy to my people Israel" (7:14). Clearly, the call to prophesy is irresistible. A powerful illustration of this compulsion is shown in Jeremiah (20):

> Yahweh's word has been the cause
>
> Of insult and derision all day long.
>
> I would say to myself, "I will not think about him,
>
> I will not speak in his name any more."
>
> But then there seemed a fire burning in my heart,
>
> Imprisoned in my bones.
>
> The effort to restrain it wearied me.

Clearly, the prophetic tradition is based on the experience of something that takes control of the normal conscious personality and needs to speak through it. The prophets themselves distinguished between what they perceived as the false prophesy of individuals who prophesy from their own "deluded dreams" as opposed to those who receive the word from Yahweh.

Apart from the content of the prophetic writings, which is not my concern, the form of prophetic utterance is similar to the form of Mr. A.'s experiment in automatic writing. What one sees from the written record is a picture of a type of person who receives ideas and motor impulses from an irresistible psychic force that seems to be of external origin. To be authentic, the prophet must reinforce the belief in an external deity in covenant with certain social groups. Could the collective needs and aspirations of a group of people crystallize into an articulate force that appropriates the nearest suitable person as a mouthpiece? A Jeremiah? An Amos? A Moses?

In every culture, and at all times, the weakness of consciousness seeks a way out of its inherent limitations. A conscious being is forced to face the profound instability of existence, not to mention the instability of her own mind. The argument here is that within our own consciousness, the source of all our woes, are also hidden depths with power to assist and support us. The prophetic tradition is one of the great forms of human dialogue with the transcendent.[177] The sage, the shaman, and the prophet open doors to transcendent guidance, and become the shapers of schools, institutions, ongoing traditions.

Diviners of Ancient Greece

Divination and the verb *to divine* are interesting words. To divine, as a verb, is to guess, to use second sight, to intuit; as an adjective, divine means godlike, heavenly, superlatively good. To divine then is what makes, reveals, or recognizes the divine. Here the causal relationship between paranormality and religiosity is patent. It comes out vividly in a book on the seer in ancient Greece by the classical scholar Michael Flower.[178]

This book has a bold thesis. According to Flower, "divination was a major system of knowledge and belief for the Greeks and was practiced in regard to every sort of important question."[179] The seer (*mantis*) was the diviner, and seership pervaded all levels of Greek society. Oracles, which were fewer in number than seers and restricted to special places and times, were also consulted for divinatory purposes. Oracles could be called mediums or prophets and acted as if they were possessed by the god who spoke through them. The handier, more pervasive seercraft used dependable systems for interpreting signs. Unlike fortune-tellers and pop psychics of modern society, Flower reminds us, the clientele of the ancient Greek seer consisted of statesmen, generals, and other accomplished citizens in the mainstream of political life.

The seer was obliged to master the technical aspect of the craft, but much more was involved, such as intuition and ecstatic utterance. Every act of divination was a complex performance, a mixture of technique and intuition. Seers and oracles sometimes faked the appearance of possession or inspiration, no doubt enhancing the dramatic effect. Despite their many obvious failures, and despite the mockery inflicted by satirists like Lucian of Samosata (b. 125 AD), the overall judgment of Greek society concerning divination was positive. "The rites of divination were not only ubiquitous in Greek society, they were also uniquely authoritative. This was true not just for the uneducated masses, but also for the elite, and not just in the archaic period, but even during the classical and Hellenistic periods."[180] How to explain this pervasive, authoritative status of divination?

The Greek seer practiced divinatory arts such as augury, the interpretation of dreams; of portents like lightning, thunder, earthquakes, eclipses; and the chance utterance of words, in fact all sorts of exceptional occurrences or stunning coincidences. It involved divination by the abnormalities of the innards of sacrificial animals. Sphagia, used on battle-lines, involved slitting an animal's throat and observing the manner in which the blood spurted out. An important technique was hepatoscopy, or divination by scrutiny of the liver. In addition, there were the great oracles at Delphi, Dodona, Olympia, and other sacred locales. There were rules the skillful diviner needed to know; for example, a bird approaching from the left is a *sinister* omen. Many techniques involved perceptually ambiguous situations that worked a bit like Rorschach imagery, designed to stimulate intuitive leaps and flashes of insight.

The seer was an aid in situations of existential crisis, at such times when habit and common sense fail in the presence of sudden obstacles. So that "divination not only provides answers to perplexing and difficult questions; it also facilitates decisive action in cases where individuals might otherwise be at a loss to act."[181] The function of divination was not to predict the future for the sake of curiosity, but to facilitate action at the junctions of life when action is unavoidable. Viewed from this perspective, some sort of "religion" is inevitable, for there will always be limits to what rule-based rationality can do and always be situations where humans have to deal with existential shock, impasse, and disorienting novelty.

It is striking that these creative people of antiquity, inventors of democracy, tragedy, comedy, satire, philosophy, logic, history, epic poetry, rhetoric, comparative mythology, political science, theory of education, etc., also used divination in every department of their lives. From the pursuit of democracy to the ventures of war, in every risky human enterprise and critical life transition, seers, sibyls, signs, and oracles were observed and deployed to assess a situation and empower action. Was there a link between the exceptional creativity of the Greeks and their skill at the *interpretative* arts of divination? A religion centered around the ability to interpret signs at all levels of life might indeed lend itself to creativity in the arts and sciences.

Flower admits that fellow scholars find the idea of divination "profoundly alien" to their rationalistic and positivistic biases. But what, specifically, was so alien? In the conclusion, he writes that it "was the seer who acted as the critical bridge between the limited and partial knowledge of mortals and the superior knowledge of the gods."[182] Alien is the idea of "superior knowledge" and the idea of "gods" as agents of such knowledge. That a seer might obtain knowledge by supernormal means is alien to the prevailing scientific mindset. The ancient Greeks apparently believed such knowledge was possible, often and consistently enough for seercraft to survive from archaic to Hellenistic times *as a mainstream institution.*

How to explain the Greeks' "genuine belief in the objective validity of divination"? Far from being credulous or slavish in their thinking, the ancient Greeks invented logic, mathematics, and philosophy. Diviners were high status professionals, competed for the best clients, made money, and often achieved fame in life or mythic eminence in literature. How to explain the high station of diviners in

Greek society? Two answers seem possible: *either* the professional seers, by sheer chutzpah and charisma, conned the most intellectually lively civilization of the ancient world for the duration of its existence *or* at least a significant part of the time the seers did impart useful advice and insight, sometimes aided by paranormal means.

In light of the *modern* evidence for paranormal cognition, I think it reasonable to suppose that the ancient seers produced *enough* paranormal cognition to explain the longevity of divination. Flower refuses to take this line, and asserts: "...clairvoyance as a psychological attribute may or may not be a characteristic of some individuals. Unfortunately, the truth or falsity of such phenomena cannot be proven"[183] That's nonsense, for well over a hundred years psychical researchers and parapsychologists have been collecting case histories and performing experiments that have done what Flower says cannot be done.

The practice of divination, widely employed in all parts of the ancient world, cannot be dismissed, and in fact it represents another form of dialogue with the transcendent. It is a mistake to identify the classical Greek as some kind of paragon of pure rationality. Much of what we might call creative irrationality pervaded the culture in many ways.[184]

All the traditional forms of practice may be seen as elaborate developments of what we saw in the Clelia experiment, all forms of *dialogue with the subliminal mind.* We should not leave out of this catalogue poets like Rimbaud, Yeats, Merrill, Blake, and many others, all inspired, and all automatists in poetic composition. In a famous letter, Rimbaud describes how he practiced making himself "clairvoyant." He summed it all up in a very short sentence: *je est un autre*. "I am an another" or "there is another I." Mr. A would have been intrigued by Rimbaud, having found "another" in himself, the seductive Clelia.

Scientific Invention and the Subliminal Mind

The psychological process we are describing has implications for all kinds of creativity, not just religious or spiritual or artistic. Myers wrote about genius based on his conception of the subliminal mind,[185] stating that creative genius can express itself in any domain of experience. That is a point worthy of noting with interest. Genius is possible in any situation where we feel, think, sense, act, will, or imagine. Any one of those modalities is capable of drawing on the wealth of the subliminal mind to an original degree that we describe as genius.

According to Myers, welding together dream and reality—the subliminal and the supraliminal parts of our psyches—is the essence of genius. Myers understood genius as the co-operation of all the strata of personality: a general coincidence of opposites, figuratively, the dance of Shiva and Shakti. Myers' idea of genius covered all aspects and situations of our mental and physical life. A "subliminal uprush," flash of inspiration, spontaneous intuition may occur in the most surprising of contexts. Epiphanies small might play out in accidental encounters with other people. Doubtless there are tales to tell of genius in raising children, sustaining a marriage, coping with horrible jobs, turning loss into spiritual gain, something ugly into beauty, failure into creative advance. Any experience may provide a platform for a sudden outpouring of genius.

Certain individuals have supernormal talents for highly abstract matters like music and mathematics. Consider the story of Ramanujan (1887-1920), perhaps the greatest Indian mathematician.[186] A self-taught prodigy born in a backwater near Madras in Southern India, he believed he owed his mathematical insights to the goddess of his local stone shrine. According to the German mathematician, Felix Klein, "mathematics has been advanced most by those who are distinguished more for intuition than for rigorous methods of proof."[187] G.H. Hardy, the distinguished mathematician from Cambridge who befriended Ramanujan, ranked Ramanujan— on a scale from one to a hundred—at one hundred for *intuitive* genius. By intuitive is meant *direct*, without sensory or logical intermediaries. Intuitions break the chain of the more familiar types of causality. They may be preceded by need, study, incubation, but when they do arrive, it is sudden, unpredictable, and complete.

Ramanujan was raised near a temple where he communed with and took counsel from a family goddess, Namagiri. It was she who wrote his formulas on his tongue and gave him equations in his dreams. T.K. Rajagopolan, who knew Ramanujan in Madras, recounts that the mathematician said "scrolls containing the most complicated mathematics used to unfold before his eyes" after dreaming of the goddess Namagiri. What amazed the experts about Ramanujan was his ability to connect the most improbable of dots; he brought together mathematical ideas remote and disconnected from one another into new coherence; in chaos he discerned order. According to E.T. Bell, Ramanujan had "all but supernatural insight"[188] into unseen mathematical relations. He is a perfect fit for Aristotle's criterion of genius being a capacity for metaphor, in which hidden connections are seen and meaning is "transferred" from one thing to another. Meaning connects, links together, transfers, etc.; there are no rules that tell you how to create metaphors or how to see connections. They turn up unpredictably anywhere, anytime; on the other hand, there are things we can do to nudge the psyche into creative furor.

In Clelia's story we observed a process that can express itself in a variety of situations and at different levels of complexity and duration. Mr. A. communed with Clelia for a mere few days. Throughout his short life, Ramanujan invoked the Dravidian goddess, Namagiri, who provided the mathematical discoveries. Ramanujan seems to have transcended technique, talent, craft, anything resembling rule-bound rationality; he simply arrived at new mathematical ideas, equations, and solutions, leaving no trail of the steps traversed. If anyone should doubt the potent reality of Myers' subliminal mind, the case of Ramanujan's Clelia, now named Namagiri, should be a clear illustration.

Ramanujan was not warmed, in spirit or in flesh, by Cambridge or by Western hospitality; he was, so to speak, a fish out of water; a believer in astrology, spirits, gods and goddesses, thrown into a culture of rationalistic stuffed shirts. Despite the awed recognition of his genius, he died at the early age of 33. The story of Ramanujan is a spectacular example of the role of the creative unconscious in science.

A book published in 1932, *Invention and the Unconscious*, by J.M. Montmasson, is replete with examples of scientists and inventors of all types and grades. Again and again, scientists are given some sudden insight or flash of inspiration that leads to a new theory or useful invention. Montmasson stresses the importance of feeling, desire, and need that drives scientific discovery.

Like Mr. A., one must be clear enough to ask the question. In April of 1802, a jubilant André-Marie Ampère, the French mathematician and physicist who is considered the father of electrodynamics, wrote:

> It was seven years ago, I proposed to myself a problem, which I had not been able to solve directly, but for which I had found by chance a solution, and knew that it was correct, without being able to prove it. The matter often recurred to my mind, and I had sought twenty times unsuccessfully for this solution. For some days I had carried the idea about with me continually. At last, *I do not know how*, I found it, together with a large number of curious and new considerations concerning the theory of probability.[189]

A similar example of eruption from the subliminal of another great mathematician, Johann Carl Friedrich Gauss, who in a letter of September 3, 1805, wrote: "At last two days ago I succeeded, not by dint of painful effort, but so to speak by the grace of God. As a sudden flash of light, the enigma was solved. For my part, I am not in a position to point to the thread that joins what I knew previously to what I have succeeded in doing." Ampere and Gauss both call special attention to what Myers referred to as the "incommensurability" between conscious effort and subliminal result, likened to the "the grace of God" by Gauss. We are back to Mr. A.'s wonder in the presence of "Clelia" baffling him with playful anagrams. And like Mr. A., and other diviners and prophets, Ampere and Gauss do make the conscious effort, do interrogate, and do have to wait for a response.

The French mathematician Henri Poincaré left some detailed accounts of his deployment of the creative unconscious. Again, the incommensurability between the conscious, working mathematician and the way the subliminal mathematician operates is notable. For a fortnight Poincareé had been groping with Fuchsian functions, playing with all sorts of combinations, but failing to achieve positive results. Then one night he broke his routine (note the spontaneity, great predictor of psi) and drank black coffee. "I could not sleep; ideas crowded in on me; they seemed to me to collide with one another, until two of them hooked together, as it were, to form a stable combination. In the morning I had established the existence of one class of Fuchsian functions, that derived from the hyper-geometric series."[190] This is rather like Mr. A.'s subliminal Clelia created out of the permutation of letters in the alphabet anagrams, concealing code that may reveal hidden meanings. Poincare was on a roll. The next day he had to take a bus to do a seminar on geology and had stopped thinking about mathematics. Then it just happened. "At the moment of putting my foot on the step, the idea occurred to me, without anything in my immediately preceding thoughts having prepared me for it, that the transformations which I have used to define Fuchsian functions were identical with those of non-Euclidian geometry."

Still working on these problems, Poincaré describes another hurdle he managed to get past by virtue of a "subliminal uprush." "Disgusted with my failure, I went for a few days' holiday to the seaside and thought of quite other matters. One day, while walking on the cliffs, the idea occurred to me, again with the same characteristics of brevity, suddenness and certitude that arithmetical transformations of indefinite ternary quadratic form were identical with those of non-

Euclidean geometry."

Poincare concludes: "What will strike you at first (in trying to understand mathematical invention) are these appearances of sudden illumination which are the manifest tokens of a long unconscious labor which has preceded them; the part played by this unconscious labor in mathematical invention appears incontestable to me, and traces will be found of it in other cases where it is less evident." The testimony of Poincare reinforces from a fresh angle the impression of the dialogical nature of transcendent process.

As Montmasson sees, sudden illumination is always preceded by conscious labor— questions, bad starts, fumblings, taking things in at random, analyzing, absorbing—and then, unexpectedly, it comes through like a finished product. Like prophets, diviners, and oracles, all in their way posing a question and getting replies that seem to come, involuntarily, from some external agency. Like Ramanujan, and as Montmasson stresses throughout his study, Poincare describes the esthetic and emotive side of mathematical creativity.

Descartes' Olympian Dreams

Known as the father of modern Western philosophy, Descartes, expounder of rationalism and mechanism, made use of dreams in his mental evolution. On November 10, 1619, he had three dreams that were life-transforming. It may come as a surprise that this hero of the scientific revolution should attach so much importance to dreams, but the historical evidence for these dreams is solid.[191] Descartes' dreams are similar to Socrates' daemon; it's curious that two of the key figures in the history of rationalism were attuned to, and guided by, psychic automatisms. Descartes' dreams, like Socrates' daemon, figured in his philosophical life, but with one big difference. Socrates' daemon was with Socrates throughout his life, until the moment of his death; Descartes' dreams produced a major impact on his method and his confidence, but the lightning struck only once for him.

On that day in November, "having gone to bed completely filled with enthusiasm, and wholly preoccupied with the thought of having found that very day the foundation of a wonderful science," Descartes had three dreams that he wrote down and commented on, producing a Little Notebook made of parchment, which was lost in the 17th century. This record of his night's extraordinary dreams he titled *Olympica*. Adrien Baillet's 1691 biography of Descartes included a close paraphrase of the *Olympica*. So we know the content of the dreams and Descartes' commentary on them.

The first two dreams were emotionally disturbing. They reflected the anxiety and disorientation that Descartes' project of radical rationalism might foster. In the first dream, he found himself walking the streets, confronted by frightening ghosts and strong winds buffeting him toward the left. Then he noticed a school and felt an evil presence threatening to seduce him.

The second dream quickly followed, and after turning to his right side he heard a loud terrifying sound he took to be thunder. He woke up, opened his eyes, and noticed sparks scattered around the room. Then the terror faded, and he slept again and this time had a different kind of dream. A mysterious book had uncannily appeared on his table. He opened and found it to be a Dictionary. Then another book appeared titled *Corpus Poetarum*, and he chanced upon a verse, "What way in life shall I follow?"

In Baillet's summary of the *Olympica,* Descartes interpreted the Dictionary to signify "all the sciences gathered together," while the *Corpus Poetarum* he took to signify the "union of Philosophy and Wisdom." By the third dream, Descartes had already begun, while still dreaming, to form his interpretations. Descartes believed his dreams came from "on high" and said that even mediocre poets might surpass the wisdom of the philosophers. "He attributed this marvel to the divinity of Enthusiasm and the strength of Imagination, which bring out the seeds of wisdom that are found in all men's minds..."

Finally, according to Baillet's summary, Descartes "was bold enough to persuade himself that it was the Spirit of Truth [God] that had wanted to open up to him the treasures of all the sciences by this dream." Descartes divined the last dream as prophetic of his own future, and it filled him with enthusiasm and confidence, as he imagined himself stepping onto the stage of world history.

The dreams appeared to come from a transcendent source, as he stated in his Notebook that "his human mind had nothing to do with them." (The poet William Blake said the same about *his* prophetic writings.) The combination of terror and exhilaration prompted a "prayer to God, so that He might make known His will to him, enlighten him, and guide him in the search for truth. He appealed to the Holy Virgin, laying before her this affair, which he considered the most important in his life." Then he vowed to go on a pilgrimage to Notre Dame of Loreto—the traveling house of Loreto I described in Chapter Two.

Dreams can point to the past and the future. Descartes was in a fever of enthusiasm over his ideas for a new method of searching for truth. But his first two dreams filled him with guilt, uneasiness, and foreboding. Descartes' new method for the acquisition of truth began with *omnia dubitando*, a systematic suspension if not destruction of all previous beliefs, going as far as doubting the existence of the external world. An apocalyptic methodology, it wants to wipe out all of history, of tradition, of accumulated wisdom and poetry, of the arts and political savoir faire, and a good deal more. This plan began with total destruction, to be followed by total rational reconstruction, beginning with the one absolute truth of the solitary ego that says *cogito*—I think and therefore I am. The disturbing dreams of ghosts, of strange winds that blew him toward his sinister side, the sound of disapproving divine thunder, and so forth, were likely the fallout from cutting himself off from his emotional roots, culture, and family.

He had rebelled against his class and the careers that were his aristocratic lot but which he recoiled from with fear and loathing—the legal, the military, the religious. Descartes felt remorse in his nightmares, but the wonderful ideas of rational method and experimental science he was devising were too enticing to resist. John Cole refers to Descartes' "egocentric rationalism." The 23 year old enjoying the solitude of his heated chamber decides he can do away with everything—not just his father's or class's authority—but any authority whatsoever. The third dream was positive, as far as Descartes was concerned, coming, he thought, from "the Spirit of Truth." The constructive potential of the new method and the third dream triumphs, and Descartes converts all the bad omens and dark images into good omens and bright signposts.

The neurologist and psychiatrist Karl Stern wrote about Descartes and his dreams,[192] reminding us that Descartes' mother died in childbirth when he was one year old; the loss left Descartes bereft of any sense of the feminine, isolating him within the confines of his pure intellect, cut off from the risk of exposure to the pains and disappointments of material life. Stern reminds us that matter and *mater* (mother) come from the same Latin root. For Stern, Cartesian dualism, rationalism, and scientism represent the spirit of anti-life and anti-femininity. The nightmarish aspect of the three dreams, the dark spirit of destruction was revelatory but sidetracked. Stern speculates that Descartes repressed his feelings of bereavement. Instead, he pursued with missionary zeal the analysis of physical nature, which laid the foundations for technology to dominate matter, that is, the mother, the matrix of our material existence.

Stern saw the fatal flaw in Descartes' personality in the way he died. It was in the dead of winter after five months of tutoring the severely intellectual Swedish Queen Cristina. Descartes was a man of refined needs and frail constitution; happiness for him was a warm bed, time to sleep, to dream, and to invite leisurely dialogue with his ideas and scientific problems. This condition his teachers at LaFleche understood; they made allowances for him and his eccentric habits. Not so Queen Cristina. Stern views the Queen as a *recognizable* cold-blooded, controlling type. She insisted on being tutored at five in the morning in the Swedish winter; she also insisted on stuffing Descartes with elaborate meats and exotic fowl, all of which disagreed with his digestive system. It took five months for him to get sick and die.

Stern's comment: "That this motherless, roaming spirit would finally succeed in maneuvering himself inextricably into the hands of the Anti-Mother! Cristina literally deprived him of the maternal triad, warmth and sleep and proper food, and thus, with the uncanny sureness of her own unconscious, caused him to die." Stern, in fact, suggests that Descartes fell prey to a self-destructive automatism.

A momentous transition was at hand, the dawning of a new philosophy and a new worldview. There was a loneliness about this quest for knowledge of mechanical nature. The haunting shadows and ghostly winds of Descartes' dreams are still with us: the reign of quantity keeps demanding from us, in ever more stealthy ways, the sacrifice of "the humanities."

Holy Spirit, Glossolalia, Serpent Handling

A very different kind of dialogue with Mind at Large involves a phenomenon akin to automatic writing, a kind of automatic speech, called *glossolalia*, or "speaking in tongues." Glossolalia is part of the Christian experience of the Holy Spirit. With early Christians, conversion involved more than accepting a new belief system, a new ethical or even eschatological code; it was about having special, exalted, inspired experiences. The Acts of the Apostles Chapter 19 records what happened when Paul arrived at Ephesus and spoke with some new disciples: "Did you receive the Holy Spirit when you believed?" he asked. The disciples said they didn't know what he was talking about. Paul gave them a demonstration: "And when Paul had laid his hands upon them, the Holy Spirit came on them, and they began speaking in tongues and prophesying." Accepting a doctrine was just one aspect of becoming a Christian; the experience of the Holy Spirit was crucial, an experience of ecstatic transformation.

Acts 2:1 describes the phenomenon of the Holy Spirit.

> And when the day of Pentecost had come, they were all together in one place. And suddenly there came from heaven a noise like a violent, rushing wind, and it filled the whole house where they

> were sitting. And there appeared to them tongues as of fire distributing themselves, and they rested on each one of them. And they were all filled with the Holy Spirit and began to speak with other tongues, as the Spirit was giving them utterance. Now there were Jews living in Jerusalem, devout men, from every nation under heaven. And when this sound occurred, the multitude came together, and were bewildered, because they were each one hearing them speak in his own language.
>
> And they were amazed and marveled, saying, "Why, are not all these who are speaking, Galileans? And how is it that we each hear them in our own language to which we were born?"

A long list follows: Parthians, Medes, Elamites, Cappadocians, Phrygians, Pamphylians, Egyptians, Lybians, and Romans. On the day of Pentecost their inspired speech, a Galilean dialect, was heard and allegedly understood in the languages of all these peoples.

There are two ways we can look at this. The first is a direct fit with the text of Acts. Each person present heard *inwardly in their own language* whatever they heard when the other spoke in melodious but meaningless tongues. We could call this an instance of *telepathic xenoglossy*; the ability to transfer specific language skills from one mind to another by telepathic means. Of course, the idea of instantly acquiring knowledge of a skill that takes weeks if not months normally to acquire only deepens the mystery.

There is perhaps a more plausible interpretation. Studies of people who speak in tongues today prove that the quasi-verbal, language-imitating, effusions are not based on known languages. The syllabic patterns of the tongue-speaker are derived from his native tongue and follow certain simple patterns. Ecstatic feelings, released from rational speech, produce a hypnotically receptive consciousness. It is easy to imagine that bystanders were caught up in the enthusiasm of glossolalia; the indefinite white noise and rolling rhythms might induce in listeners the hallucination of words telepathically influenced.

Glossolalia differs sharply from *xenoglossy*. What the speaker in tongues creates is a kind of omni-language of ambiguity and misdirection in which linguistic music supersedes semantic function. Glossolalia, the language of angels, destroys and transcends all local meaning. In its inarticulate wisdom, tongue-speaking resonates with the mystical idea that the supreme truth is ineffable. Glossolalia destroys meaning and converts language into ecstatic music.

Glossolalia is referred to in the same breath with prophecy by Saint Paul. But glossolalia is the opposite of prophecy, which uses powerful truth-speaking words to critique power and evokes images of a transformed future. Glossolalia goes beyond all syntactical references; it creates a language of abstract spiritual feeling. Beyond agreement and disagreement, glossolalia is a kind of exuberant suicide of science and philosophy. In their place, it offers radical freedom from the tyranny of all finite forms of meaning.

At the nameless core of tongue-speaking, we return to ancient times suggesting Dionysian spirituality or perhaps Zen satori or the annihilation (*fana*) of Sufi mysticism. What all these practices share is a facility for transcending the constraints of rational language. On the other hand, also reminiscent of Dionysiac ecstasy is the image of "taking up serpents" and the ability to ingest deadly substances like lye, strychnine, and kerosene, and not be "hurt" by them.

The practice of snake-handling and the Pentecostal movement grew up in America, first in California, around the dawn of the twentieth century. It is the most Hollywoodian of miracles; the spectacle of a man ecstatically waving deadly snakes in his hands or a woman downing a cocktail of kerosene. Between 1880 and 1926 twenty-five new churches were established in America that called themselves Holiness, referring to the state of being possessed by the Holy Spirit. Becoming Pentecostal was about reviving the magical origins of Christianity.[193]

Handling serpents was one of the featured practices of the new

Pentecostal churches but has been in decline for the last 20 years. The Pentecostal experience is about regeneration of the whole personality; it is accomplished by means of immersion or baptism in the *hagia pneuma*, the holy or healing spirit.

Serpent handling and drinking poison are "signs" that one has entered a new dispensation, a radically new form of consciousness. The practices are dangerous and occasionally end in death. In Thomas Burton's study of the phenomenon,[194]many cases are cited, often of leading figures, who die; there is no quantitative analysis or much medical data, though at least a hundred cases are on record. Snake-handling and related practices are outlawed in all states but West Virginia, but man's law has failed to prevent the saints from doing their experiments in Pentecostal holiness. Snake-handling, with its reckless disregard for human life, might seem like religious psychopathy. Most Christians neither practice nor condone "taking up serpents."

There is an impressive bibliography on the subject and YouTube abounds in short films of serpent handlers in action along with interviews of them. Among the scholarly treatments, anthropologist Weston LaBarre seems tone-deaf to the transcendent aspirations of the snake-handler and reduces the phenomenon to a Freudian struggle to master the repressed phallic propensities of serpent-handlers!

Burton, however, summarizes studies of serpent-handlers that find them to be normally functioning human beings with jobs and families from different economic and educational backgrounds. Some of their practices are undoubtedly risky, sometimes with fatal results, but so are the practices of race-car drivers, people who feel obsessed to climb Mt. Everest, and patriotic soldiers who volunteer for dangerous missions.

Handling serpents is admittedly high on the list of risky rites of self-transformation; it must, however, be seen against the whole Pentecostal project and the goal of total spiritual regeneration. The prophets pictured a time in history when nature would be transformed and the "lion will lie down with the lamb," as it were. Ritual death of the ego, along with rigorous, even life-threatening efforts at self-mastery, have traditionally been part of the human quest for transcendence. There is, in fact, a condition for the proper way of engaging in this extreme form of spiritual experimentalism. Ordinary faith in scripture is not sufficient; there must be what Pentecostals call "the anointment of the Holy Spirit." Anointment refers to the altered state of possession by the Holy Spirit. Not being "anointed," in the proper altered state, is one explanation of cases of snake bite fatality. Here is how Brother Bud Gregg of Morristown, Tennessee, put it: "…when the Spirit of the Lord begins to take control of your body, he begins to move you around and he preaches through you and speaks in tongues through you, he begins to shout through you, or whatever, something else greater than a man begins to take control of a man's body and begins to do these things—that's what they call the anointing of God." [195] And that's what we can call voluntary psychophysical possession.

This description exemplifies the same form of experience as Mr. A's experiment in automatic writing reported by Myers. There is the same basic sense of being in the presence of, and controlled by, what seems "something else greater than a man." In a wildly evolved development of the principle, the Holy Ghost-Spirit becomes a more available "Clelia" for believers. Being anointed for the Pentecostal means being occupied by an externally invasive psychical power, something numinous, something like kundalini energy, which, like Myers' subliminal uprush, can affect *every* modality of consciousness.

Here is how Anna Prince, also of Tennessee, the daughter of Ulysses Prince, well known serpent handler and sister to Robert Prince who died from a ritual snake-bite, describes the anointment: Anna lived, and believed in, the faith. But she seems to have been horrified by the extreme gestures, which killed her brother. On the other hand, she deeply appreciates the value of the anointment:

> It's a spiritual trancelike strand of power linking humans to God; it's a burst of energy that's refreshing, always brand new; it brings

> on good emotions. One is elated, full of joy. You know you're right with God, totally in tune with God; every thing is right with every one on earth. It's a delicious wonderful feeling going through your body; it's a roar of happiness; you want to laugh, jump. It's a power surge that is near to a light, electrical shock and a sexual orgasm simultaneously felt, but it is not sexual or electrical, just a similar sensation. It's close to sensual without being sexual; it's loving, not making love. Love surges through the body in waves; one knows no enemies; one wants to dance in happiness or hug somebody. It's addicting – once you feel it you want to feel it again; it causes people who get hooked on the feeling to band with others who feel it in order to get a bigger and deeper high. One feels akin to God, free of guilt, pain, shame or "pull downs" that often plague a person. The anointed one is nearly unearthly for a few minutes....The anointing is catching; once it begins, it often runs around the room from person to person – sometimes whole buildings of people are hit at once, and everyone stands up and begins moving around the building and performing comical antics of leaping, shouting, dancing, praising God. Adults revert to uninhibited children...[196]

This is an unusually revealing document. It contradicts every cliché and stereotype one might entertain about an Appalachian serpent-handler. "It knows no enemies." In this sense, Anna presents a reality that is profoundly non-fundamentalist. It is not afraid of expressing itself in whatever way it sees fit. It is not guilt-ridden, not anti-body, not anti-life, not anti-joy. The irrepressible impetus to trance dance is as reminiscent of Dionysus as it is of St. Joseph of Copertino; the use of surging sexual and electrical metaphors suggests as much tantric-engendered or kundalini energies as it does the *hagia pneuma*.

That this is an ecstatic and releasing experience at its anointed core and not a doctrinally manipulated experience; that, in its core, it is radically anti-fundamentalist is given away when she says, "everything is right with everyone on earth." This is the simple spirit of oneness that the mystic knows and that has left behind all dualistic divisiveness, and with that, the terrible inanities of the fundamentalist cast of mind. She observes that the state of mind she so exults in is psychically contagious, and admits that getting others to join her in ecstasy will deepen her own ecstasy. The *hagia pneuma* is a kind of force field, a little like ball lightning that bounces from person to person, prompting the performance of "comical antics of leaping, shouting, dancing..." which aspire to unearthliness "for a few minutes." This could well describe a kind of divine "commedia del Arte."

It seems clear to me that the Pentecostal experience involves much more than repressed sexuality. In any case, so what if it chooses to sublimate and transform sexual energy into new spheres of consciousness? Thomas Burton states that the people he studied who handled poisonous serpents and drank poisons were otherwise rational human beings, but that "believers evoke a 'power' that works for them."[197] We of course have a name for the kind of power able to accomplish things normally impossible—*psychokinesis*.

All this is contained in germ by the story of Mr. A. carrying on a colloquy with his own dream. We can learn to communicate with the normally hidden side of ourselves. In this experiment, the conscious part interrogates the larger but submerged mind, the awareness that exists below the threshold of biological alertness. The entire transaction assumes a personal form, and "Clelia" is born. The question posed, one elicits a response: the seed of a god, a personification of the unknowable part of ourselves. In every case, there is need, tension, a *cri de coeur*, a petition, a shuddering wail. And that sets into motion a response, if one picks up on the signal. In every example, a moment arrives that creates an opening for something to break through.

Saint Paul found an inscription on a statue in Athens dedicated to the unknown God. "For as I passed along, and observed the objects of your worship, I found also an altar with this inscription: 'To an *Unknown God.*'" (Acts: 17:23). Whoever made the inscription seemed to recognize there might be something else than the known, the named sources of the divine, something deeper than the named forms. The question we've posed is about actively engaging with this greater reality.

We began this chapter with an experiment that became the nucleus of our discussion—in which a Mr. A. found himself conversing with an intelligence apparently external to himself. The big idea in this chapter is about harboring within us intelligent and powerful beings of unknown provenance. The Other lurks inside our own mental space. In the story of Mr. A, we catch a glimpse of this. Mr. A.'s encounter with Clelia resembles in form the transcendent automatisms of major figures in history and expands the sense of what may lie within ourselves.

The data we have presented suggest that behind our routine life scenarios a greater mind may be exerting effects on us in curious, often ambiguous, but sometimes spectacular ways. This greater mind may respond to our calls, our questions, or intrude upon, get entangled with, or take possession of our lives, perhaps briefly, sometimes radically and invasively.

I think it impossible to say what the outer limits of the miraculous potentials are or how they will manifest in the future. The miracles discussed point toward potential changes in human nature. Detached from their doctrinaire assumptions, they help us imagine possible trends of human evolution. Miracles—beginning with the obvious miracle of consciousness—are weighty grounds for rejecting the creed of physicalism. They enlarge the universe of possible experience and broaden the horizons of the future.

Last Words: Beyond Science and Religion

We have tracked and confronted various reports of miracles, tried to peel away cultural accretions, and zeroed in on the empirical core. Miracles, the most extreme forms of paranormal phenomena, stretch our imagination of the possible. Encased often but not all the time in religious settings, access can be convoluted and awkward. What I found reveals a dizzying picture of super-human abilities, a mirror image of what I believe is latent in us all, by virtue of our being grounded in the substratum of the One Mind—the working hypothesis of this book.

I'm sure we all agree that the ethos of science forbids us to ignore challenging data, even if it seems blatantly to contradict the materialist creed. David Hume's refusal to confront the stunning miraculous data right before him was twofold: his rigid conception of the uniformities of nature but also his dread of ratifying anything in any way supportive of "Papism" or organized religion. Political bias warped his own philosophical faith in the primacy of experience. Hume's essay on miracles itself contains all the evidence needed to refute his dogmatic thesis that miracles are impossible.

Miracles, as we have defined them in terms of their extra-physicality, exist. That's the first conclusion. The evidence is available in various forms and all we've done is examined some interesting samples. There's a great deal out there waiting to be explored, understood, and perhaps deployed in the art of living our lives. The human mind seems to possess a range of abilities we do not understand. That should give us pause. What does all it all mean? An entire sphere and dimension of mind-stretching experiences? What, I would like to know, are these extraordinary abilities *for*? It's hard to think of them as being just evolutionary quirks or flukes. The feeling of strangeness persists, and I ask: Why psi? Why these tantalizing forays into magic, the "impossible," the transcendent?

In the chapter 'Things to Do with Miracles,' we discussed ways that science and religion may benefit from tackling miracle data: science by engaging new and intellectually challenging phenomena and religion by seeing how the data is at least consistent with some general religious beliefs such as life after death, the power of prayer, and the reality of a greater mind. The chapter discusses four variables conducive to what William Blake called "living by miracle"—calm conviction, deep introversion, unrelenting focus, and relaxed spontaneity.

In the next two chapters, we asked what the miracle data say about what it means to be human. Two big ideas emerged from my review of the phenomena in question. According to the hypothesis of Mind at Large, the data permit us to expand the concept of our everyday mind to encompass apparent extraphysical abilities, spaces, and entities. The data, in my view, allow us to move theoretically from a brain-derived personal mind to a mind grounded in a transpersonal reality, a mind at large, endowed with superpowers, examples of which we covered in the preceding chapters—things extrasensory, psychokinetic, and mystical.

But now we choose not to stand paralyzed in awe before this Great Mind whose existence we infer from so many transcendent phenomena, but in the next and last chapter—"Dialogue with The Transcendent"—we carry the exploration to the next step. Reason and matters of fact have led us to hypothesize the existence of one great mind, and we now want to ask whether it is possible to engage with this transcendent mind? But of course, we can! Whether by chant, rite, art, prayer, fasting, meditation, solitude, psychedelics, and so on, humans have always sought to contact and gain favor from higher, wiser, and more powerful beings assumed, hoped or variously sensed as real and possibly interested in us. The results of this perennial experimentalism have been encoded cross-culturally in the semiotics of other worlds, of gods and goddesses, angels and demons and aliens, and all manner of psychospiritual personnel.

In focusing on miracles, I wanted to tell a story that was not quite about science or religion but something perhaps more akin to metaphysical performance art. All the extraordinary phenomena can of course be construed in the context of science and religion, but I believe that miracles exist for reasons that transcend their roles in organized religion and systematic science. Stripped down to their essence, to what they imply about human capacities, miracles represent the spontaneous unfolding of the creative energies of nature through the most conscious and versatile form of life on earth.

I like to think of these gathered tales of miracles as a kind of commons of extraordinary experiences, a place to throw off assumptions that might oppress us unnecessarily and arbitrarily, a theater where the play of imagination is given free reign. The various reported charisms and *siddhis*, the whole dictionary of supernormal phenomena, taken together suggest a picture of a possible superhuman being with remarkable powers over physical reality, matched, we must hope, by comparably evolved mental and spiritual powers.

So why then do we have these abilities? Three interwoven possibilities come to mind, all of considerable interest. They may be foreshadowing either our yet to be realized terrestrial evolutionary potential, or our postmortem evolutionary potential, or both. It appears that all the miracle data are future oriented. We might, if we chose to, see them as pointing to the next stage of our biological evolution *or* of our post-biological existence.

There is, after all, something very strange about these "abilities," which may not be the right word at all. Our miracle powers are mainly untrainable, not producible on demand, and largely useless in this life. They're totally unpredictable and arbitrary in the way they manifest. Their effect may just be a metaphysical tease and wake-up call. Their fuller meanings perhaps will be revealed when we part company with terrestrial life, and our extrasensory abilities, normally recessive, spring into their full potential activity. In death, we are stripped down to our extrasensory selves and powers (should it be), fully released into the medium of disembodied (think dreamlike) existence.

The next world will of necessity be constituted by telepathy, clairvoyance, and psychokinesis; and our experience of time will be strange, more intimate and more awe-inspiring, likely to widen our mental view of things *or* terrify us into flight, dislocation, and disembodied myopia. For some the new environment may turn out to be quite disconcerting. The *Tibetan Book of the Dead* is an instruction manual on how to minimize the first shocks and terrors of being thrust into a disembodied afterworld as a consequence of dying.

The difficult thing, we are told, is recognizing that the frightening scenes and monsters of the next world are projections of our own unconscious. To be able to do that may require a little previous practice in our embodied life. The bad news is that we are likely to terrify ourselves into doing the worst possible thing: turn into a peeping Tom (or Jane) in order to select a means of transportation back into the world of the living, thus having to endure the calamity of reincarnation.

The full complement of these psychic powers, viewed synoptically, prompt us to radically expand our concept of mind. With the Upanishads, the Neo-Platonists, Renaissance magicians, and German idealists, via Aldous Huxley's Mind at Large, we hypothesize the ultimate source and repository of the mental universe and its elusive, unpredictable, miraculous powers.

History shows that curious, racked and daring individuals have sought to connect with the greater mind, so secretive and temperamental; our species has learned to name and experiment in many fields of consciousness with the enigmatic Being of beings. The great mind is very far and very close, and we are more or less permeable to the hidden recesses of ourselves. So the call of the Delphic oracle to "know ourselves" has a more urgent ring to it than perhaps ever before.

Why such emphasis on the exotic and interior worlds when the world out there is coming apart? My answer to this question is both practical and metaphysical. Whatever our beliefs and opinions, whatever our status in life and society, each of us has to live with ourselves. We have to live with our perceptions, feelings, beliefs, our shifting memories, and uncertainties. We can't escape being ourselves. There is no way out of our consciousness. We can't escape our moment to moment consciousness. Wherever it is, there you are.

Miracles point toward a new realm of freedom from the constraints of physical reality. I began with a quote from philosopher and science fiction writer Olaf Stapledon, who tells the story of human evolution into the far future until he reaches the time of the 15th race of Men and Women of Neptune. Stapledon seems to agree with Frederic Myers on the central role of telepathy in the next stage of human evolution.

"Partly through the immense increase in mutual understanding, which resulted from telepathic rapport, partly through improved co-ordination of the nervous system, the ancient evil of selfishness was entirely and finally abolished from the normal human being," he wrote in *Last and First Men* (1930). His vision is not one of linear progress but of constant growth and change, self-destruction and self-renewal. An endless spiral journey, not one magnificent climax.

The phenomena we have discussed tell us that a transformation of human nature and human society is possible. The need for an evolutionary leap forward is now, I'm afraid, before we're totally engulfed by catastrophe. We are the performers in the theater of the world where the next stage of human evolution will play out, act by act, scene by scene. We are a long way from the abolition of evil and the telepathic rapport that Olaf Stapledon imagined in the future human on Neptune. But who knows? The moment in history may arrive when we come together in the One Mind; it will be a convergence of spirit that transforms the planet. What seems miraculous today will become the new common sense.

Endnotes

1 Pierre Mathieu (2006) *Histoire des Miraculés et de Convulsionnaires de Saint-Medard*. Elibron Classics.

2 Schapiro, H (1964) *Medieval Philosophy*, New York: Modern Library, p.85.

3 James, W. (1900) *Human Immortality: Two Supposed Objections to the Doctrine*. Houghton, Mifflin.

4 McGinn, C. (1999) *The Mysterious Flame: Conscious Minds in a Material World*. New York: Basic Books.

5 See Kelly, E. (2007) *Irreducible Mind: Toward a Psychology for the 21st Century*. Rowman & Littlefield.

6 For a close examination of the difficulties, see Alan Gauld, Chapter 4 in *Irreducible Mind.*

7 See David Presti's *Foundational Concepts of Neuroscience* (2016) for a lucid account of the tricky relationship between mind and brain.

8 Herbert, N. (1985) *Quantum Reality: Beyond the New Physics*. Anchor Books.

9 Woodward, K. (1996) *Making Saints.* New York: Touchstone.

10 Mathieu. P.F (2006) *Histoires Des Miraculés et Des Convulsionnaires de Saint-Médard*. Paris: Elibron Classics.

11 See the 2018 National Geographic special, *The Story of Mary*.

12 For a detailed account of the miracle and the extraordinary art it produced, see Catherine D. Harding (2004) *Guide to Chapel of the Corporal of Orvieto Cathedra*l. Orvieto Cathedral.

13 Feilding, E. (1963) The Case of the Abbe Vachere. In *Sittings with Eusapia Palladino & Other Studies*. University Books, pp. 299-314.

14 The following seven cases up to the case in Italy, 1994, are draw from the internet, condensed.

15 Source: *Washington Post; USA Today*.

16 Source: New York *Newsday*.

17 Grosso, M. (1995) *The Millennium Myth: Love and Death at the End of Time.* Quest Books.

18 Woodward, K. (2000) *The Book of Miracles.* Touchstone, p. 315.

19 For a fascinating account of miracles in the Middle Ages, see Benedicta Ward (1982) *Miracles and the Medieval Mind*. University of Pennsylvania Press.

20 Ward, B. (1982) Ibid., p. 2.

21 Elkin, A.P. (1945/1977) *Aboriginal Men of High Degree*. New York: St. Martin's Press.

22 See *Secrets of Aboriginal Healing* (2013) by Gary Holz with Robbie Holz. Rochester, Vermont: Bear & Comapany.

23 Alexandra David-Neel, (1965) *Magic and Mystery of Tibet.* Penguin Books.

24 Grosso, M. (2012) *Soulmaking: Uncommon Paths to Self-Understanding.* Charlottesville: Anomalist Books.

25 Andrew Lang (1898) *The Making of Religion.* London: Longman.

26 David Barker, 1978, Psi phenomena in Tibetan culture, in *Research in Parapsychology*: Scarecrow Press: Metuchen, NJ, pp. 52-55.

27 Thurston, H. (1952) *Physical Phenomena of Mysticism*; Murphy, *Future of the Body*; Scott Rogo, *Miracles*; Treece, *The Sanctified Body;* Treece, *Nothing Short of a Miracle*; J.C. Cruz, *Relics* and *The Incorruptibles*.

28 Thurston, ibid.

29 Dingwall, E.(1962), *Some Human Oddities*. University Books, p.30.

30 Pastrovicci, A. (1980) *St. Joseph of Copertino*. Tan Books, p. 35.

31 See for the fullest account in English, my *The Man Who Could Fly* and *Wings of Ecstasy*.

32 Peers, E. A. (1960) *The Autobiography of St Teresa of Avila.* Image Books.

33 Thurston, H. 1951 *The Physical Phenomena of Mysticism*. London: Burns Oates, p. 12.

34 The literature on Eusapia Palladino is extensive, having been investigated by many learned peoples from all over Europe. See, for example, Dingwall, E. (1962) *Very Peculiar People*, pp.178-215.

35 Dingwall, E. (1962), ibid. pp.119-144

36 See Ian Wilson's (1989) *Stigmata.*

37 Thurston, H. (1952) *Physical Phenomena of Mysticism*, p. 44.

38 Thurston, ibid. p. 133.

39 Thurston, ibid. p.146

40 Thurston, ibid, p. 181

41 McClenon, J. (1994) *Wondrous Events: Foundations of Religious Belief.* University of Pennsylvania Press.

42 Burkan,T. (2001) *Extreme Spirituality.* Hillsboro, Beyond Words Publishing.

43 Thurston, ibid. p.196.

44 Thurston, ibid. p. 216.

45 Thurston, ibid, p. 218.

46 Steiner, J. (1966) *Therese Neumann: A Portrait Based on Authentic Accounts, Journals and Documents.* Staten Island: Alba House.

47 See the article on *manna* in Tyndale's *New Bible Dictionary.*

48 See Thurston's discussion of food making marvels.

49 See Brewer's erudite *Dictionary of Miracles.*

50 Rogo, D. S. *Miracles: A Parascientific Inquiry into Wondrous Phenomena.* New York: Dial Press, p. 145.

51 M.J. Vuillemin, (1908) "Report on the 'Hailstone Medallions," *Annals of Psychical Science* 7, 426-428.

52 M.Sage, (1909) “The alleged miraculous hailstones of Remiremont.” *Society for Psychical Research,* 21, 405-435.

53 Rogo, ibid. p.156.

54 L.Garlaschelli, F. Ramaccini, S.Della Sala (1994) *The Blood of Saint Januarius*, Chemistry in Britain., 30,2, p.123.

55 Biondi, M. (2005) *Trasformazioni.* Oscar Mondadori.

56 I have relied on a series of unpublished papers by Kenneth Batcheldor.

57 Ustinova, Y. (2018) *Divine Mania: Alteration of Consciousness in Ancient Greece*. New York: Routledge

58 Otto, W. F. (1965) *Dionysus: Myth and Cult.* Indiana University Press, pp. 98-99. This account of the ancient movement that had such an impact on later developments wants readers to understand that at least some of the alleged miracles were real.

59 Quoted in *Relics* by Joan Carroll Cruz, p.174.

60 See Noreen Renier’s (2008) *A Mind for Murder: The Real-Life Files of a Psychic Investigator*. Hampton Roads Pub.

61 Geoffrey Ashe, *Man, Myth, and Magic*, p. 2350.

62 Denton, W. (1866/1988) *The Soul of Things: Psychometric Researches and Discoveries.*

63 See the extraordinary case of Claire Sylvia: https://listverse.com/2016/05/14/10-organ-recipients-who-took-on-the-traits-of-their-donors/

64 Tribbe, F. (1983) *Portrait of Jesus?: The Illustrated Story of the Shroud of Turin.* New York: Stein & Day.

65 Robin Lane Fox, (1986), *Pagans and Christians*, Harper & Row: New York, p. 375.

66 See my *Frontiers of the Soul: Exploring Psychic Evolution* (1992) Quest Books, Ch.5 on St. Paul's conversion.

67 Ibid. Fox, p. 613

68 Edward Gibbon, (1891), *History of Christianity*, Eckler, p. 600.

69 Ibid., p. 601.

70 Jody Brant Smith (1984) *The Image of Guadalupe: Myth or Miracle*? Image Book.

71 See Thurston's discussion and the book by Joan Carroll Cruz, *The Incorruptibles*.

72 Thurston, ibid. p, 234.

73 See Yogananda's *Autobiography of a Yogi* (1975).

74 Stephen Grosso (1996) *Experiencing Lourdes: An Intimate View of the Miraculous Shrine and its Pilgrims*. Ann Arbor, Michigan: Charis.

75 Carty, C.M. (1973) Padre Pio *The Stigmatist*. Tan Books, p.160.

76 Bertrin, G. (1908) *Lourdes a History of its Apparitions and Cures*, available on www.facsimilepublisher.com.

77 Keener, C. (2011(*Miracles: The Credibility of the New Testament Accounts.* Vol. 1, p. 2. .

78 See Duffin, J. (2011) *Medical Miracles: Doctors, Saints, and Healing in the Modern World.* Oxford University Press.

79 See especially Larry Dossey's *Healing Words* (1993) HarperSanFrancisco and *Be Careful What You Pray For—You Just Might Get It*. (1997) HarperSanFrancisco.

80 See my essay "The Parapsychology of God" in Charles Tart's anthology *Body Mind Spirit: Exploring the Parapsychology of Spirit* (1997).

81 Taimni, I.K. (1961) *The Science of Yoga*. A Quest Book, p. 357

82 Bayle, P. (2000) *Various Thoughts on the Occasion of a Comet*. State University of New York Press.

83 Of Miracles, (1748/1955) Sec. 10, *An Inquiry Concerning Human Understanding*, New York: Library of Liberal Arts.

84 Dingwall, Eric (1962), *Some Human Oddities*, New York: University Books, pp.68-90.

85 Mathieu, P., (1864/2006) *Histoire Des Miraculés et des Convusionnaires de Saint-Medard*, Paris: Elibron Classics.

86 Knox, R.A., 1950, *Enthusiasm: A Chapter in the History of Religion*. Oxford University Press, pp. 372-388.

87 Domenico Bernini, (1722)*Vita Del Giuseppe da Copertino*, Roma.

88 *Inquiry Concerning Human Understanding*, p.88.

89 It is well known that Thomas Jefferson produced his own emended version of the New Testament. He accomplished this feat on his own in a few evenings. He deleted all references to miracles. Jefferson believed Jesus was the greatest social philosopher of the ancient world. He couldn't possibly have walked on water or healed anybody.

90 Parts of this work have been translated into English, and there is an excellent study by Renee Haynes's about the Enlightenment Pope, see *Philosopher King: The Humanist Pope: Benedict XIV*. (1970).

91 See, for example, William Roll (1972) *Poltergeists*, documented case histories of invisible entities wreaking all manner of impossible havoc on mundane reality. Real metaphysical entertainment.

92 Ellenberger, H.F. (1970). *The Discovery of the Unconscious*. New York: Basic Books; also Crabtree, A. (1993). *From Mesmer to Freud: Magnetic Sleep and the Roots of Psychological Healing*. Yale University Press.

93 See Ebenezer Cobham Brewer's encyclopedic *A Dictionary of Miracles*.

94 See William Walsh, *Our Lady of Fatima* (1954).

95 Kamell, YG; Jacksonm JP; Jackson, RS (1996) *A Lady of Light Appears in Egypt: The Story of Zeitoun*: Colo.

96 Laurentin, R. & Joyeux, H. (1987) *Scientific and Medical Studies on the Apparitions at Medjugorje*. Dublin: Veritas. Klimek, D. (2018) *Medjugorje and the Supernatural*. Oxford University Press.

97 See Karlis Osis & Erlendur Haraldsson (1977) *Deathbed Visions*.

98 See Nandor Fodor's article in the *Encyclopedia of Psychic Science* (1966) University Books, pp. 392-395.

99 See Braude, S. (1991)*The Limits of Influence*. London: Routledge. A thorough and careful analysis of psychokinetic phenomena.

100 Erlendur on Sai Baba

101 Murphet, H. (1973) *Sai Baba: Man of Miracles.* Samuel Weiser, Inc.; Haraldsson, E (1987) *Miracles Are My Calling Cards*.

102 Padre Pio of Pietrelcina: *Acts of the First Congress of Studies Padre Pio's Spirituality*, Ed. Gerado Di Flumeri, San Giovanni: Rotondo, 1972.

103 Ibid.

104 Agostino of San Marco in Lamis (1975) Diario. SGR.

105 Schug, J, (1975) *Padre Pio: He Bore the Stigmata*, Huntington, Indiana: Our Sunday Visitor, p.55.

106 Boniface, E. (1971) *Padre Pio Le Crucifie*. Paris: Nouvelles Editions.

107 Parente. A. (1983) *Send Me Your Guardian Angel.* San Giovanni Rotundo.

108 *The Voice of Padre Pio*, Vol.5, No. 3, 1975, pp.14-15.

109 Carty, C.M.(1973) *Padre Pio the Stigmatist*. Rockford, Ill.: Tan.

110 See Scott Rogo's book, *Miracles* (1982), which documents the prodigies of these two saints.

111 Ruffin, B. (1982) Padre Pio: *The True Story.* Huntington, Ind. Our Sunday Visitor.

112 This was the expression Padre Pio used to explain how he bilocated when someone asked. Other times he just said God sent him places. The interesting point is he himself continually affirmed the reality of his excursions through hyperspace. For another angle on the evidence, his confreres often heard him giving absolution or otherwise conversing with invisible or far-off beings.

113 See Ruffin, ibid., p.266.

114 *The Friends of Padre Pio.* Vol. 2, pp. 14-16.

115 Neihardt, L. (1972) *Black Elk Speaks*. Pocket Books.

116 Barker, D. (1978) Psi phenomena in Tibetan culture. *Research in Parapsychology.* Metuchen: Scarecrow.

117 See Carty's account of this, pp. 57-58.

118 Wallace, A. R. (1878) *Miracles and Modern Spiritualism.* London: Spiritualist Press.

119 *Creative Evolution*, by H. Bergson.

120 Boniface, E. Ibid.

121 I intend a double sense for *conceit*, as referring to a conception or idea, but also the popular derivative, so and so it "conceited," that is, overestimates his virtues.

122 I prefer the shorter *telic* to the six-syllabled *teleological*, related to "final causation."

123 See for an overview Tim Martin, *Essential Surrealists* (2000) Paragon Publishing.

124 Andre Breton, see his *Automatic Message*.

125 To gain insight from a physicist into how dream and waking spaces might conceivably fuse for brief periods of time, see Bernard Carr's chapter, "Hyperspatial Models of Matter and Mind," in *Beyond Physicalism,* ed. E. Kelly, E.Crabtree, and P.Marshal.

126 For a critique of the idol of *uniformity*, see Paul Feyerabend's *Farewell to Reason.*

127 U.M.Schneede, (1973) *Surrealism: The Movement and the Masters*, p.19, Abrams Publishers: New York.

128 Anna Balakian (1970), *Surrealism: The Road to the Absolute.* New York: Dutton.

129 See the Introduction by Robert Graves to *The Golden Ass* by Apuleius, in the Graves translation.

130 See Hans Vaihinger's 1911 remarkable *The Philosophy of 'As If'.*

131 Batcheldor, K. J, (1963) *Psychokinesis, Resistance, and Conditioning*. Unpublished Manuscript.

132 Blake, *Auguries of Innocence.*

133 See Jean-Pierre de Caussade (1975) Image Books.

134 Mishra, R. (1964), *Fundamentals of Yoga*, p. 24.

135 Honorton, C, (1977) "Psi and internal attention states." *Handbook of Parapsychology*, ed. Wolman, pp.435-472.

136 See "Patanjali's Yoga sutras and the siddhis," in *Beyond Physicalism*, pp, 315-348.

137 Woodward, K. (2000) *The Book of Miracles*, p.151.

138 Schmidt, H. (1987) "The strange properties of psychokinesis." *Journal of Scientific Exploration*, I , 103-118.

139 See Ernesto De Martino's book *The World of Magic* (1971) that makes the case for the reality of "magic."

140 Radin, D. (2018) *Real Magic.* New York: Harmony Books.

141 Ruth Murry Underhill (1938) *Singing for Power: The Song Magic of the Papago Indians.*

142 Underhill, R. M. (1938/1968) *Singing for Power: The Song Magic of the Pagago Indians*. NY: Ballantine.

143 See Kirkpatrick Sale, "The Illusion of Saving the World" in *Counterpoint*, Sept. 26, 2019.

144 Gurney, E. (1888) "Experiments in Hypnotism," *Proceedings*, Vol.5, p.3.

145 Palmer, J. (1978) Extrasensory perception: research findings. In Krippner, S. Ed. *Advances in Parapdychological Research.* 2. New York, Plenum.

146 See Andre Breton's *Automatic Message* (1990) London: Atlas Press.

147 Eco, U. 1986.

148 Mabille, P. (1998) *Mirror of the Marvelous*. Inner Traditions, p. 45.

149 Article in *Chronicle of Higher Education.*

150 See the Ingersoll Lecture (1900 *Human Immortality: Two Supposed Objections to the Doctrine*.

151 See *Original Self*, (2001) p. 87.

152 David-Neel, A. (1967) *The Secret Oral Teachings of Tibetan Buddhist Sects*. City Light Books, p. 71.

153 Aldous Huxley, *The Doors of Perception* and *Heaven and Hell,* New York: Harper & Row, 1963, p. 23-24,

154 Bergson, H. (1913) Presidential Address. *Proceedings for the Society of Psychical Research*, 27, pp. 157-175.

155 *Human Personality*, V.2, p. xix.

156 Sidgwick, *Crisis Apparitions.*

157 Kirk&Raven, p.205 (ibid).

158 H.H. Price, on prayer (ibid).

159 Dossey on *One Mind* and *Healing Words*

160 See Honorton, C. (1977) "Psi and Internal Attention States." *Handbook of Parapsychology*. Wolman, Ed.

161 Targ, E. (1997) "Evaluating Distant Healing: A Research Review." *Alternative Therapies.*

162 Batcheldor, K. J. (1983) "Contributions to the theory of PK from sitter-group work." *Journal of the American Society of Psychical Research.* 78, pp. 105-122.

163 Saltmarsh, H. F. (1938) *Foreknowledge*. London: Bell & Son's.

164 See my *Soulmaking*, Anomalist Books.

165 Ibid. Saltmarsh, p.52.

166 Jonathan Bricklin (2015) *The Illusion of Will, Self, and Time: William James Reluctant Guide to Enlightenment.*

167 Huxley, A. (1970) *The Perennial Philosophy*. Harper, NY, p.28, London: 1938.

168 Myers, "On A Telepathic Explanation of Some So-Called Spiritualistic Phenomena". *Society for Psychical Research, Proceedings*, 1884, pp.217-237.

169 See, for example, Sonu Shamdasani, *Automatic Writing and the Discovery of the Unconscious*, Spring, Vol.54, (1993), pp. 100-131.

170 Prince, W.F. (1927/1924) *The Case of Patience Worth*. University Books.

171 For an extraordinary account of the creative subconscious, see Carl Du Prel's *The Philosophy of Mysticism* (1977) Arno Press, especially Chapter 5, "Dream a Physician."

172 Myers, *Proceedings*,1885, p.24, Automatic Writing, II.

173 Anita Muhl (1963). *Automatic Writing.* New York, Helix Press.

174 *The Autobiography of Benvenuto Cellini,* (Trans. By John Addington Symonds) Sun Dial Press: New York, 1927, pp.260-262.

175 Flournoy, p.102.

176 See *New Bible Dictionary*, p. 979.

177 See my book *The Millennium Myth: Love and Death at the End of Time* (1995).

178 Flower, M. (2008) *The Seer in Ancient Greece*. University of California Press.

179 Ibid.p.2.

180 Ibid., 104-105.

181 Ibid, p.74.

182 Ibid, p.240.

183 Ibid, p.6.

184 Dodds (1946) *The Greeks and the Irrational.*

185 See chapter on genius in *Irreducible Mind.*

186 Robert Kanigel (1991) *The Man Who Knew Infinity: A Life of the Genius Ramanujan*. Pocket Books: New York.

187 Ibid, p.226.

188 Ibid, p.280.

189 Montmasson, J. P. (1932) *Invention and the Unconscious*. Harcourt, p. 76.

190 Montmasson, ibid. p. 80.

191 John Cole, *The Olympian Dreams &Youthful Rebellion of Rene Descartes*, 1992, University of Illinois Press: Chicago.

192 Karl Stern, *The Flight from Women*, Noonday: New York, 1965, 75-105.

193 Charles, W. (1977) *Like a Mighty Army Moves the Church of God*. Cleveland, Tenn. Church of God Publishing.

194 Thomas Burton (1993) *Serpent Handling Believers*. Knoxville: The University of Tennessee Press.

195 Ibid.

196 Burton, ibid., p.140.

197 Ibid., p.135.

Index